YAHSHUA ✡
The Messianic Hope

RAY LOOKER

YAHSHUA - THE MESSIANIC HOPE

(The King James Bible was used in the preparation of this book)

http://www.raylooker.com

ISBN-13: 978-1482701678
ISBN-10: 1482701677

Copyright: 2005 - Floyd R. Looker, Jr.

All Rights Reserved

No part of this book may be reproduced, stored in a retrieval system, or transmitted by any means, electronic, mechanical, photocopying, recording, or otherwise, without written permission from the author.

MESSIANIC BOOKS

By Dr. Ray Looker

In Defense of Truth

Replacement Theology

The Messianic Prayer Book, 2d Ed.

Judeo-Christianity, 2d Ed.

Messianic Code of Jewish Law

Messianic Guide to the Epistles

Yahshua - The Messianic Hope

(http://www.raylooker.com)

DEDICATED TO MY BELOVED

CHIANNA

FOREWORD

"Yahshua - The Messianic Hope," is compiled from the King James translation of the Gospels of Matthew, Mark, Luke, John, and some references from the books of Acts of the Apostles, and Revelation. The first of a two-fold purpose of this rendering is to present a chronological sequence of the life and works of Yahshua, son of David, Son of Yahweh.

The second aspect of this presentation is to remove the anti-Semitic influences in the presentation of the Gospels. Now, as we read these Scriptures, we see that the Jews were following Yahshua by the thousands. So, who was plotting to kill Yahshua? The Chief Priests, the Pharisees, and the Scribes were instrumental in advancing this idea. It was they who sought to kill Yahshua, not the Jewish people. The Jewish people came from all over Israel, and from foreign lands to hear His message, to receive healings, deliverances, and blessings.

To say, or even imply, that The Jewish people were trying to kill Yahshua grew out of the Gentile separation from the Church of Jerusalem.

Initially the Nicolaitan rebellion split from the Council of Jerusalem and began to systematically assimilate Babylonian religious practices. In their desire to create a religion separate from Judaism, the Catholic religion, which grew out of the Nicolaitan rebellion, sought to create a new religion as far removed from Judaism as possible. A breach was created that has never yet been healed. The more the Gentiles assimilated pagan practices, and departed from the teachings of Scripture, the less the Jewish Believers wanted anything to do with them.

The entire purpose of this presentation of the Gospel is to return to the truth of Scripture, and to analyze it within the context of New Testament times, and Jewish thought and custom. It is our intent to present a chronological history of the life and works of Yahshua in a way that becomes more enjoyable to the casual reader, the new Believer, and Jews who wish to discover Yahshua in a way that becomes more enjoyable, and less threatening.

The task of sorting through four books in order to understand Yahshua's life has caused many to set the story aside as too complex. Hopefully, we have made it easier to comprehend the life of Yahshua, and surely, by removing the anti-Semitic bias, we have made it possible for the Jewish people to read the story without being offended by anti-Semitic dialogue. Instead of presenting an "us and them" situation, we hope to better reveal the inherent aspects of our unity in the Messiah.

In Judaism the concept of the Messiah is basic to Jewish Theology and belief. It is found in the writings of the prophets, which are filled with references to the Messiah. At least 60 times daily Orthodox Jewish prayers are full of requests to the Messiah, and throughout history our Jewish ancestors have prayed for the coming of the Messiah. Jewish customs, such as breaking of the glass at the wedding ceremony, and saying at the end of the Passover Seder service, "Next Year in Jerusalem" are expressions of Jewish belief in and anticipation of the coming of the Messiah.

The coming of the Messiah is expected to be a culmination and crowning stroke to bring world peace and holiness. This coming of the Messiah is expected to free the Jewish people from all servitude to foreign nations, to rebuild the Holy Temple in Jerusalem and gather all Jews to Israel. Peace and prosperity will be universal, and all nations will serve and worship Yahweh. The Messiah will reveal Righteousness in every facet of our lives.

The Jewish people are taught that they can hasten the coming of Messiah by doing more "Mitzvoth", learning more "Torah" and praying for His coming. These "Mitzvoth" involve helping others through economic assistance, physical help, words of encouragement, kindness and emotional support, reading and studying the "Torah" more often, and by putting more meaning and spiritual completeness into all their actions.

The story of Yahshua, who is the Messiah, is truly unique in that He more than anyone else in history, has met all the requirements of the prophetic vision for the Messiah. His life has been an example of the peace that passes all understanding. The life He lived revealed Righteousness in His life.

In reaching out to touch the lives of first century Jews, He alone has transformed the nations by His example and in His promises of eternal reward and inner peace. The story begins in Bethlehem of Judea, as revealed by the prophets of old.

The author has presented as complete a picture of the life of Yahshua as presented in the Gospels and has attempted to include all aspects of each of the Gospel writers' views of what happened. Any omissions are strictly mistakes of the author and were never intended.

The result of over 70 years of experience and training, in the universities and at the feet of Yahshua, has taught the author much about the universal doctrines of the Messiah which transcend denomination barriers and allows the reader to look beyond the horizon to see how the Bride must prepare herself for the coming of the Lord. This book is a beginning of the preparation for the soon coming reign of the Messiah.

Ray Looker - (5760) & January 2013

CONTENTS

Messianic Books by Ray Looker

Foreword

Chapter I	1
Chapter II	16
Chapter III	36
Chapter IV	54
Chapter V	71
Chapter VI	88
Chapter VII	106
Chapter VIII	133
Chapter IX	159
Chapter X	172
Chapter XI	189
Chapter XII	212
Biography	228

CHAPTER I

In the beginning was the Word, and the Word was with Yahweh, and the Word was Yahweh. The same was in the beginning with Yahweh. All things were made by Him and without Him was not anything made that was made. In Him was life and the life was the light of men, and the light shined in darkness, and the darkness comprehended it not. He was in the world, and the world was made by Him, and the world knew Him not.

He came to His own, His own received Him not. But as many as received Him, to them gave He power to become the sons of Yahweh, even to them that believe on His Name. Who were born, not of blood, nor of the will of the flesh, nor of the will of man, but of Yahweh.

And the Word was made flesh and tabernacled among us, (and we beheld His glory, the glory as of the only begotten of the Father), full of grace and truth. There was in the days of Herod, the king of Judea, a certain priest named Zechariah, of the course of Abijab, and his wife was of the daughters of Aaron, and her name was Elizabeth.

And they were both righteous before Yahweh, walking in all the commandments and ordinances of Yahweh blameless.

They had no child, because Elizabeth was barren, and they both were well stricken in years. And it came to pass, that, while he executed the priest's office before Yahweh in order of his course, according to the custom of the priest's office, his lot was to burn incense when he went into the Temple of Yahweh. And a whole multitude of people were praying without at the time of the burning of the incense.

There appeared to Zechariah an angel of Yahweh standing on the right side of the Altar of Incense. When Zechariah saw the angel he was troubled and fear fell upon him. But the angel said to him, "Fear not, Zechariah, for your prayer is heard, and your wife Elizabeth shall bear you a son, and you shall call his name John."

"You shall have joy and gladness of heart, and many shall rejoice at his birth. He shall be great in the sight of the Lord, and shall drink neither wine nor strong drink, and he shall be filled with the Holy Spirit, even from his mother's womb."

"Many of the children of Israel shall he turn to Yahweh their God. And he shall go before Him in the spirit and power of Elijah, to turn the hearts of the fathers to the children, and the disobedient to the wisdom of the just, to make ready a people prepared for the Lord".

Zechariah said to the angel, "How shall I know this? I am an old man and my wife is well stricken in years." The angel said to him, "I am Gabriel, I stand in the presence of Yahweh. I have been sent to speak to you, and to show you these glad tidings. Behold, you shall be dumb and not able to speak, until the day that these things shall be performed, because you did not believe my words, which will be fulfilled in their season.

The people waited for Zechariah and marveled that he tarried so long in the Temple. And when he came out, he could not speak to them, and they perceived that he had seen a vision in the Temple, for he beckoned to them, and remained speechless.

It came to pass, that, as soon as the days of his ministration were accomplished, he departed to his own house. After those days his wife Elizabeth conceived, and hid herself five months, saying, "Thus has Yahweh dealt with me in the days wherein He looked on to take away my reproach from among men."

In the sixth month, the angel Gabriel was sent from Yahweh to a city of Galilee, named

Nazareth, to a virgin espoused to a man whose name was Yosef, of the house of David, and the virgin's name was Miriam, and the angel came in to her, and said, "Hail highly favored, Yahweh is with you, blessed are you among women." When she saw, she was troubled at his saying, and cast in her mind what manner of salutation this should be.

The angel said to her, "Fear not, Miriam, for you have found favor with Yahweh. Behold, you will conceive in your womb, and bring forth a son, and you will call His Name Yahshua. He will be great, and shall be called the Son of the Highest, and Yahweh will give to Him the throne of His father David, and He shall reign over the house of Jacob forever, and of His Kingdom there shall be no end."

Then said Miriam to the angel, "How can this be seeing I know not a man?" The angel answered and said to her, "The Holy Spirit shall come upon you, and the power of the Highest shall overshadow you. Therefore that Holy thing which shall he born of you shall he called the Son of Yahweh."

"Your cousin Elizabeth has also conceived a son in her old age, and this is the sixth month with her, who was called barren. With Yahweh nothing shall be impossible." Miriam said, "Behold the handmaid of Yahweh, be it to me according to your word." The angel departed from her.

Miriam arose in those days, and went into the hill country with haste, into a city of Judah, and entered into the house of Zechariah, and saluted Elizabeth. And it came to pass, that, when Elizabeth heard the salutation of Miriam, the babe leaped in her womb, and Elizabeth was filled with the Holy Spirit, and she spoke out with a loud voice, and said, "Blessed are you among women and blessed is the fruit of your womb."

"What is this to me that the mother of my Lord should come to me? As soon as the voice of your salutation sounded in mine ears, the babe leaped in my womb for joy. Blessed is she that believes, for there shall be a performance or those things which were told her from the Lord."

Miriam said, "My soul does magnify the Lord, and my spirit has rejoiced in Yahweh my Savior. For He has regarded the low estate of His handmaiden, for, behold, from henceforth all generations shall call me blessed. For He that is mighty has done to me great things, and holy is His Name."

"His mercy is on them that fear Him from generation to generation. He has showed strength with His arm, He has scattered the proud in the imaginations of their hearts. He has put down the mighty from their seats and exalted them of low degree. He has filled the hungry with good things, and the rich He has sent empty away. He has helped His servant Israel, in remembrance of mercy, as He spoke to our fathers, to Abraham, and to his seed forever."

Miriam abode with Elizabeth about three months, and returned to her own house. Now Elizabeth's full time came that she should be delivered, and she brought forth a son. Her neighbors and her cousins heard how Yahweh had showed great mercy upon her, and they rejoiced with her.

It came to pass, that on the eighth day they came to circumcise the child, and they called him Zechariah, after the name of his father. His mother said, "Not so, but he shall be called John." And they said to her, "There is none of your kindred that are called by this name." And they made signs to his father, how he would have him called. And he asked for a writing table, and wrote, saying, "His name is John." And they all marveled.

Zechariah's mouth was opened immediately, his tongue loosed and he spoke, and praised Yahweh. Fear came on all that dwelt round about them, and all these sayings were noised abroad throughout all the hill country of Judea. All they that heard laid it up in their hearts, saying, "What manner of child shall this be?" And the hand of Yahweh was with him.

His father Zechariah was filled with the Holy Spirit and prophesied saying, "Blessed is Yahweh, the Lord God of Israel, for He has visited and redeemed His people, and has raised up a horn of salvation for us in the house of His servant David, as He spoke by the mouth of His holy prophets, which have been since the world began."

"That we should be saved from our enemies, and from the hand of all that hate us; to perform His mercy to our fathers, and to remember His holy covenant the oath which He swore to our father Abraham, that He would grant to us, that we, being delivered out of the hand of our enemies, might serve Him without fear, in holiness and righteousness before Him, all the days at our lives."

"You, child, shall be called the prophet of the Highest, for you shall go before the face of the Lord to prepare His ways, to give knowledge of salvation to His people by the remission of their sins, through the tender mercy of Yahweh our God; whereby the dayspring from on high has visited us, to give to them that sit in darkness and the shadow of death, to guide our feet into the way of peace." The child grew and waxed strong in spirit, and was in the deserts until the day of his showing to Israel.

Now the birth of Yahshua was on this wise. When His mother Miriam was espoused to Yosef, before they came together, she was found with child of the Holy Spirit. Then Yosef, her husband, being just and not willing to make her a public example was minded to put her away privacy.

While he thought on these things, behold, the angel of Yahweh appeared to him in a dream, saying, "Yosef, son of David, fear not to take to you Miriam your wife, for that which is conceived in her is of the Holy Spirit. She shall bring forth a son, and you shall call His Name Yahshua, for He will save His people from their sins."

Now this was done, that it might be fulfilled which was spoken of the Lord by the prophet, saying, "Behold, a virgin shall be with child, and shall bring forth a son, and they shall call His Name Immanuel which being interpreted is, 'Yahweh is with us.'

Yosef being raised from sleep did as the angel of Yahweh had bidden him, and took to him his wife, and knew her not until she had brought forth her firstborn son, and he called His Name Yahshua.

And it came to pass in those days, that there went out a decree from Caesar Augustus, that the entire world should be taxed. This taxing was first made when Cyrenius was governor of Syria. And all went to be taxed everyone into his own city.

Yosef also went up from Galilee, out of the city of Nazareth, into Judea, to the city of David, which is called Bethlehem (because he was of the house and lineage of David) to be taxed with Miriam his espoused wife, being great with child.

So it was that while they were there the days were accomplished that she should be delivered. And she brought forth her firstborn son, wrapped Him in swaddling clothes, and laid Him in a manager, because there was no room for them in the inn.

There were in the same country shepherds abiding in the field, keeping watch over their flocks by night. And, lo, the angel of Yahweh came upon them, and the glory of Yahweh shone round about them, and they were quite afraid. And the angel said to them, "Fear not, for, behold, I bring you good tidings of great joy, which shall be to all people. For to you is born this day in the city of David a Savior, who is the Messiah."

"This is a sign to you, you shall find the baby wrapped in swaddling clothes, lying in a manger." And suddenly there was with the angel a multitude of the heavenly host praising Yahweh, and saying, "Glory to Yahweh in the highest, and on earth peace, goodwill toward men."

It came to pass, as the angels were gone away from them into heaven, the shepherds said one to another, "Let us go to Bethlehem, and see this thing which is come to pass which Yahweh has made known to us."

They came with haste, and found Miriam and Yosef, and the babe lying in a manger. When they had seen they made known abroad the saying which was told there concerning this child. All they that heard wondered at those things which were told them by the shepherds. Miriam kept all these things, and pondered in her heart. And the shepherds returned, glorifying and praising Yahweh for all the things that they had heard and seen, as it was told to them.

When eight days were accomplished for the circumcising of the child, His Name was called Yahshua, which was so named of the angel before He was conceived in the womb. When the days of her purification according to the law of Moses were accomplished, they brought him to Jerusalem, to present to Yahweh (As it is written in the Law of Yahweh, "Every male that opens the womb shall be called holy to Yahweh.") and to offer a sacrifice according to that which is said in the Law of

Yahweh, "A pair of Turtledoves, or two young pigeons."

And behold, there was a man in Jerusalem, whose name was Simeon and the same man was just and devout, waiting for the consolation of Israel, and the Holy Spirit was upon him. It was revealed to him by the Holy Spirit, that he should not see death, before he had seen Yahweh's Messiah.

He came by the Spirit into the Temple, and when the parents brought in the child Yahshua, to do for Him after the custom of the Law, then took he Him up in his arms, and blessed Yahweh, and said, "Lord, now let Your servant depart in peace according to Your word, for mine eyes have seen Your salvation, which You have prepared before the face of all people, a light to lighten the Gentiles, and the glory of Your people Israel"

Yosef and Miriam His mother marveled at these things which ware spoken of Him. And Simeon blessed them, and said to Miriam, His mother, "Behold, this is set for the fall and rising again of many in Israel, and for a sign which shall be spoken against, (Yea, a sword shall pierce through your own soul also) that the thoughts of many hearts may be revealed."

And there was one Anna, a prophetess, the daughter of Phanuel, of the tribe of Asher, she was of a great age, and had lived with a husband seven years from her virginity, and she a widow of about four score and four years, which departed not from the Temple but served with fasting and prayers night and day.

She coming in that instant gave thanks likewise to Yahweh, and spoke of Him to all of them that looked for redemption in Jerusalem. And when they had performed all things according to the Law of Yahweh they returned to Galilee, to their own city Nazareth. And the child grew, and waxed strong in spirit, filled with wisdom, and the grace of Yahweh was upon Him.

Now when Yahshua was born, in Bethlehem of Judea in the days of Herod the king, behold, there came wise men from the east to Jerusalem, saying, "Where is He that is born King of the Jews? For we have seen His star in the east, and have come to worship Him."

When Herod the king had heard, he was troubled and all Jerusalem with him. He gathered all the chief priests and scribes of the people together, he demanded of them where the Messiah should be born. They said to him, "In Bethlehem of Judah, as it is written by the prophet, 'And you Bethlehem of the land of Judah are not the least among the princes of Judah. For out of you shall come a governor, that shall rule my people Israel.'"

Then Herod, when he had privily called the wise men, inquired of them diligently what time the star appeared he sent them to Bethlehem, and said, "Go and search diligently for the young child. And when you have found Him, bring me word again, that I may come and worship Him also." When they had heard the king, they departed.

The star, which they saw in the east, went before them, until it came and stood over where the child was. When they saw the star, they rejoiced with exceeding great joy. When they came into the house, they saw the young child with Miriam his mother, and fell down, and worshipped Him.

When they opened their treasures they presented to Him gifts, gold, and frankincense, and myrrh. And being warned of Yahweh in a dream that they should not return to Herod, they departed into their own country another way.

When they had departed, behold, the angel of Yahweh appeared to Yosef in a dream, saying, "Arise, and take the young child and His mother, and flee into Egypt, and be there until the death of Herod. That it might be fulfilled which was spoken of Yahweh by the prophet, saying, 'Out of Egypt have I called my son.'"

Then Herod, when he saw that he was mocked of the wise men, was exceeding wroth, and sent forth, and slew all the children that were in Bethlehem, and in all the coasts thereof, from two years old and under, according to the time which he had diligently inquired of the wise men.

Then was fulfilled that which was spoken by Jeremiah the prophet, saying, "In Ramah there was a voice heard, lamentation, weeping, and great mourning. Rachel weeping for her children, and would not be comforted, because they are not."

When Herod was dead, behold, an angel of Yahweh appeared in a dream to Yosef in Egypt, saying, "Arise, and take the young child and His mother and go into the land of Israel. For they are dead which sought the young child's life." And he arose, and took the young child and His mother, and came into the land of Israel.

But when he heard that Archelaus did reign in Judah in the room of his father Herod, he was afraid to go thither. Notwithstanding being warned of Yahweh in a dream he turned aside into the parts of Galilee and dwelt in a city called Nazareth. Now His parents went to Jerusalem every year at the Feast of the Passover.

When Yahshua was twelve years old they went up to Jerusalem after the custom of the Passover Feast. When they had fulfilled the days, as they returned Yahshua tarried behind in Jerusalem which Yosef and His mother knew not. But they, supposing Him to have been in the company, went a day's journey. And when they sought Him among kinsfolk and acquaintance they found Him not so they turned back again to Jerusalem seeking Him.

It came to pass, that after three days they found Him in the Temple, sitting in the midst of the doctors, both hearing them, and asking them questions. All that heard Him were astonished at His understanding and His answers.

When, they saw Him, they were amazed. His mother said to Him, "Son, why have you dealt thus with us? Behold your father and I have sought you sorrowing." And He said to them, "How is it that you sought me? Do you not know that I must be about my Father's business?"

They did not understand the saying which He spoke to them. But His mother kept all these sayings in her heart. And Yahshua increased in wisdom and stature, and in favor with Yahweh and man.

CHAPTER II

Now in the fifteenth year of the reign of Tiberius Caesar, Pontius Pilate being governor or Judea, and Herod being Tetrarch of Galilee, and his brother Philip Tetrarch of Abilene, Annas and Caiaphas being the high priests, the Word of Yahweh came to John the son of Zechariah in the wilderness.

John came into all the country about Jordan, preaching the baptism of repentance for the remission of sins, saying, "Repent for the kingdom of heaven is at hand." This is he that was spoken of by the prophet Isaiah, saying, "The voice of one crying in the wilderness, prepare the way of the Lord, and make his paths straight. Every valley shall be filled, and every mountain and hill shall be brought low. And the crooked shall be made straight, and the rough ways made smooth. All flesh will see the salvation of Yahweh."

The same John had his raiment of camel's hair, and a leather girdle about his loins. And his meat was locusts and wild honey. Then went out to him from Jerusalem, and all Judea, and the region round about Jordan, and were baptized of him in the river Jordan, confessing their sins.

John said to the multitudes, to the Pharisees and to the Sadducees that came forth to be baptized of him, "O generation of vipers who has warned you to flee from the wrath to come? Bring forth fruits worthy of repentance, and begin not to say within yourselves, 'We have Abraham to our father,' I say to you that Yahweh is able of these stones to raise up children to Abraham. And now also the axe is laid to the root of the trees. Every tree which brings not forth good fruit is hewn down and cast into the fire."

The people asked him, saying, "What shall we do then?" He answered and said to them, "He that has two coats let him impart to him that has none, and he that has meat, let him do likewise."

Then came also publicans to be baptized, and said to him, "Master, what shall we do?" And he said to them, "Exact no more than that which is appointed you." The soldiers likewise demanded of him, saying, "What shall we do?" He said to them, "Do violence to no man, neither accuse falsely and be content with your wages."

As the people were in expectation and all men mused in their hearts concerning John as to whether he was the Messiah or not and certain leaders of the Temple sent priests and Levites from Jerusalem to ask him, "Who are you?" And he confessed, and denied not but confessed, "I am not the Messiah."

They asked him, "What then, are you Elijah?" And he said, "I am not." "Are you that prophet?" He answered, "No." Then said they to him, "Who are you? That may give answer to them that sent us. What do you say of yourself?" He said, "I am the voice of one crying in the wilderness, make straight the way of the Lord, as said the prophet".

They which were sent were of the Pharisees. They asked him, and said to him, "Why do you baptize then, if you are not the Messiah, nor Elijah, neither that prophet?" John answered them saying, "I indeed baptize with water. But there stands one among you, whom you know not, He it is, who coming after me is preferred before me, and is mightier than I, whose shoe-laches I am not worthy to unloose, He shall baptize you with the Holy Spirit and fire. Whose fan is in His hand, and He will thoroughly purge His floor, and will gather the wheat into His garner. But the chaff He will burn with fire unquenchable."

Many other things in his exhortation he preached to the people. These things were done in Bethabara beyond Jordan, where John was baptizing. Yahshua began to be about thirty years of age, and it came to pass in those days, that Yahshua came from Nazareth of Galilee to Jordan to John, to be baptized of him. But John forbade Him saying, "I have need to be baptized of you, and you come to me?"

Yahshua answering said to him, "Suffer it now, for thus it becomes us to fulfill all righteousness." Then he suffered Him. And Yahshua, when He was baptized, went up straightway out of the water. The heavens were opened to Him and a voice from heaven, saying, "This is My beloved Son, in whom I am well pleased."

Yahshua, being full of the Holy Spirit, returned from Jordan, and immediately the Spirit drove Him into the wilderness to be tempted of the devil. He was there in the wilderness forty days tempted of Satan, and was with the wild beasts. The angels ministered to Him. When He had fasted forty days and forty nights, He was afterward hungry.

The Tempter came to Him, and said, "If you are the Son of Yahweh, command that these stones be made bread." Yahshua answered and said, "It is written, man shall not live by bread alone, but by every Word that proceeds out of the mouth of Yahweh.

The devil took Him up to Jerusalem, and set Him on a pinnacle of the Temple, and said to Him." If you are the Son of Yahweh, cast yourself down from thence. It is written, 'He shall give His angels charge concerning you'. And in His hands they shall bear you up, lest at any time you dash our foot against a stone." Yahshua answering said to him, "Again, it is written, 'you shall not tempt Yahweh your God.'"

The devil took Him up into an exceedingly high mountain, showed to Him all the kingdoms of the world and the glory of them in a moment of time, and said to Him, "All of these things and all this power will I give you, and the glory of them. For it is delivered to me, and to whomsoever I will, I give it."

Yahshua answered and said to him, "Get behind me Satan, for it is written, you shall worship Yahweh your God, and Him only shall you serve." When the devil had ended all the temptations, he departed from Him for a season, and the angels came and ministered to Him.

The next day John seeing Yahshua coming to him, and said, "Behold the Lamb of Yahweh, which took away the sin of the world. This is He of whom I said, "After me comes a man which is preferred before me. He was before me, and I knew

Him not. But that He should be made manifest to Israel, therefore am I come baptizing with water."

John bare record, saying, "I saw the Spirit descending from heaven like a dove, and it abode upon Him. And I knew Him not, but He that sent me to baptize with water, the same said to me, 'Upon whom you shall see the Spirit descending, and remaining on Him, the same is Him which baptizes with the Holy Spirit.'"

I saw, and bare record that this is the Son of Yahweh." Again the next day after, John stood, and two of his disciples. Looking at Yahshua as He walked, he said, "Behold the Lamb of Yahweh."

Two disciples heard him speak, and they followed Yahshua. Then Yahshua turned, and saw them following, and said to them, "What do you seek?" They said to Him, "Rabbi, (which is to say, being interpreted, Master,) where do you dwell?" He said to them, "Come and see."

They came and saw where He dwell, and abode with Him that day. For it was about the tenth hour. One of the two which heard John and followed Him was Andrew, Simon Peter's brother. He first found his own brother Simon, and said to him, "We have found the Messiah."

He brought him, to Yahshua. And when Yahshua beheld him, He said, "You are Simon the son of Jonah. You shall be called Cephas", which is by interpretation, a stone.

Yahshua returned in the power of the Spirit into Galilee. There went out a fame of Him throughout the region round about. He taught in their synagogues, being glorified of all. As He walked by the Sea of Galilee, He saw Simon and Andrew his brother casting a net into the sea for they were fishermen. Yahshua said to them, "Come after me, and I will make you fishers of men." Straightway they forsook their nets, and followed Him.

When He had gone a little further He saw James of Zebedee, and John his brother, who also were in the ship mending their nets. Straightway He called them, and they left their father Zebedee in the ship with the hired servants, and went after Him.

The day following, Yahshua would go forth into Galilee, and finding Philip, and said to him, "Follow me." Now Philip was of Bethsaida, the city of Andrew and Peter. Philip, finding Nathanael said to him, "We have found Him of whom Moses, in the Law and the prophets, did write, Yahshua of Nazareth the son of Yosef." Nathanael said to him, "Can there any good thing come out of Nazareth?" Philip said to him, "Come and see."

Yahshua saw Nathanael coming to Him, and said of him, "Behold, an Israelite indeed, in whom is no guile" Nathanael said to Him, "From where do you know me?" Yahshua answered and said to him, "Before Philip called you, when you were under the fig tree, I saw you." Nathanael answered and said to Him, "Rabbi, you are the Son of Yahweh. You are the King of Israel."

Yahshua answered and said to him, "Because I said to you, I saw you under the fig tree you believe? You shall see greater things than these." He said to him, "Verily, verily, I say to you, hereafter you shall see heaven open, and the angels of Yahweh ascending and descending upon the Son of Man."

On the third day there was a marriage in Cana of Galilee. And the mother of Yahshua was there, and both Yahshua was called, and His disciples, to the marriage. When they wanted wine, the mother of Yahshua said to Him, "They have no wine." Yahshua said to her, "Woman, what have I to do with you? Mine hour is not yet come."

His mother said to the servants, "Whatever He says to you do it." There were set there six water pots of stone, after the manner of purifying, containing two or three firkins each. Yahshua said to them, "Fill the water pots with water." And they filled them up to the brim.

He said to them, "Draw out now, and bear to the governor of the feast." And they bare it. When the ruler of the feast had tasted the water that was made wine, and knew not where it came from (but the servants who drew the water knew) the governor of the feast called the bridegroom and said to him, "Every man at the beginning sets forth good wine. When men are drunk then they set forth that which is worse. You have kept the good wine until now."

This beginning of miracles did Yahshua in Cana of Galilee, and manifested forth His glory, and His disciples believed on Him. Yahshua went about all Galilee, teaching in their synagogues and preaching the gospel of the kingdom, and healing all manner of sickness and all manner of disease among the people.

His fame went though out all Syria. And they bought to Him sick people that were taken with various kinds of diseases and torments, and those who were lunatic, and those that had the palsy. And He healed all of them.

Seeing the multitudes, He went up into a mountain, and when He was set, His disciples came to Him, and He opened His mouth, and taught them, saying,

"Blessed are the poor in spirit, for theirs is the Kingdom of Heaven."

"Blessed are they that mourn, for they shall be comforted. Blessed are the meek, for they shall inherit the earth."

"Blessed are they which do hunger and thirst after righteousness, for they shall be filled."

"Blessed are the merciful, for they shall obtain mercy. Blessed are the pure in heart, for they shall see Yahweh."

"Blessed are the peacemakers, for they shall be called the children of Yahweh."

"Blessed are they which are persecuted for righteousness' sake, for theirs is the Kingdom of Heaven."

"Blessed are you, when men shall revile you, and persecute you, and shall say all manner of evil against you falsely, for my sake. Rejoice and be exceeding glad for great is your reward in Heaven, for so persecuted they the prophets which were before you."

"You are the salt of the earth, but if the salt have lost his savor, wherewith shall it be salted? It is thenceforth good for nothing, but to he cast out, and to is trodden under foot of men."

"You are the light of the world. A city that is set on a hill cannot be hid. Neither do men light a candle and put it under a bushel but on a candlestick and it gives light to all that are in the house."

"Let your light so shine before men, that they may see your good works, and glorify your Father which is in heaven."

"Think not that I have come to destroy the Law or the prophets, I have not come to destroy, but to fulfill. For verily I say to you, till heaven and earth pass, one jot or one tittle shall in no wise pass from the Law, until all is fulfilled."

"Whoever shall break one or these least commandments and shall teach men so, he shall be called the least in the Kingdom of Heaven. But whoever shall do and teach the same shall be called great in the Kingdom of Heaven."

"For I say to you, that unless your righteousness shall exceed the Scribes and Pharisees you shall in no case enter into the Kingdom of Heaven."

"You have heard that it was said by them of old time, 'You shall not kill, and whoever shall kill shall be in danger of the judgment.' But I say to you, that whoever shall say to his brother, "Raca" shall be in danger of the council. But whoever shall say, 'You fool,' shall be in danger of hell fire."

"If you bring your gift to the altar, and there remember that your brother has an anything against you, leave there your gift before the altar, and go your way, first be reconciled to your brother, and then come and offer your gift."

"Agree with your adversary quickly, while you are in the way with him, lest at any time the adversary deliver you to the judge, and the judge deliver you to the officer, and you be cast into prison. Verily I say to you, you shall by no means come out until you have paid the uttermost farthing."

"You have heard that it was said by them of old time, you shall not commit adultery. But I say to you, that whoever looks on a woman to lust after her has committed adultery with her already in his heart."

"If your right eye offends you, pluck it out, and cast it from you, for it is profitable for you that one of your members should perish, and not that your whole body should be cast into hell."

"If your right hand offends you, cut it off, and cast it from you, for it is profitable for you that one of your members should perish, and not that your whole body should be cast into hell."

"It has been said, whoever shall put away his wife, let him give her a writing of divorcement, but I say to you, that whoever shall put away his wife, saving for the cause of fornication, causes her to commit adultery, and whoever shall marry her that is divorced commits adultery."

"Again, you have heard that it has been said by them of old time, you shall not forswear yourself, but shall perform to Yahweh your oaths. But I say to you, Swear not at all, neither by heaven, for it is Yahweh's throne, nor by the earth, for it is His footstool, neither by Jerusalem, for it is the city of the Great King."

"Neither shall you swear by your head, because you cannot make one hair white or black. But let your communication be yea, yea, nay, nay, for whatever is more than these comes of evil."

"You have heard that it has been said, an eye for an eye, and a tooth for a tooth, but I say to you, that you resist not evil, but whoever shall smite you on your right cheek, turn to him the other also."

"If any man will sue you at the law, and take away your coat, let him have your cloak also. And whoever shall compel you to go a mile, go with him twain. Give to him that asks of you, and from him that would borrow of you turn not away."

"You have heard that it has been said you shall love your neighbor and hate your enemy. But I say to you love your enemies, bless them that curse you, do good to them that hate you, and pray for them which despitefully use you, and persecute you, that you may be the children of your Father who is in heaven."

"He makes His sun to rise on the evil and on the good and sends rain on the just and on the unjust. If you love them which love you, what reward do you have? Do not even the publicans the same?"

"If you salute your brethren only, what do you more? Do not even the publicans so? Be therefore perfect, even as your Father which is in heaven is perfect. Take heed that you do not your alms before men, to be seen of them. Otherwise you have no reward of your Father which is in heaven."

"When you do alms, do not sound the trumpet before you, as the hypocrites do in the synagogues and in the streets, that they may have glory of men. Verily I say to you, they have their reward. But when you do alms, let not your left hand know what your right hand does, that your alms may be in secret, and your Father which sees in secret shall reward you openly."

"When you pray, you shall not be as the hypocrites, for they love to pray standing in the synagogues and in the corners of the streets, that they may be seen of men. Verily I say to you, they have their reward. But you, when you pray, enter into your closet, and when you have shut your door pray to your Father which is in secret and your Father which sees in secret shall reward you openly."

"When you pray, use not vain repetitions, as the heathen. For they think that they shall be heard for their much speaking. Be not like them because your Father knows what things you have need of even before you ask Him."

"After this manner therefore pray, "Our Father who is in heaven, Hallowed is Your Name. Your kingdom come Your will be done in earth, as it is in heaven. Give us this day our daily bread, and forgive us our debts, as we forgive our debtors. Lead us not into temptation, but deliver us from evil. For Yours is the Kingdom, and the Power, and the Glory, forever and ever - Amen."

"If you forgive men their trespasses, your heavenly Father will also forgive you. But if you forgive not men their trespasses, neither will your Father forgive you your trespasses."

"Moreover when you fast, do not be as the hypocrites of a sad countenance for they disfigure their faces that they may appear to men to fast. Verily I say to you, they have their reward."

"When you fast, anoint your head, and wash your face. That you appear not to men to fast, but to your Father which is in secret. And your Father which sees in secret shall reward you openly."

"Lay not up for yourselves treasures upon earth, where moth and rust doth corrupt, and where thieves break through and steal. But lay up for yourselves treasures in heaven, where neither moth nor rust doth corrupt, and where thieves do not break through nor steal. Where your treasure is there will your heart be also."

"The light of the body is the eye. If your eye is single, your whole body shall be full of light. But if your eye is evil, your whole body shall be full of darkness. If the light that is in you is darkness, how great is that darkness."

"No man can serve two masters. Either he will hate the one and love the other. Or else he will hold to the one, and despise the other. You cannot serve Yahweh and mammon. Therefore I say to you, take no thought for your life, what you shall eat, or what you shall drink. Nor yet for your body, what you shall put on."

"Is not the life more than meat, and the body than raiment? Behold the fowls of the air. They sow not, neither do they reap, nor gather into barns. Yet your heavenly Father feeds them. Are you not much better than they? Which of you by taking thought can add one cubit to his stature?"

"Why do you take thought for raiment? Consider the lilies of the field, how they grow. They toil not, neither do they spin. And yet I say to you that even Solomon in all his glory was not arrayed like one of these. Wherefore, if Yahweh so clothe the grass of the field, which today is, and tomorrow is cast into the oven, shall He not much more clothe you, O you of little faith?"

"Take no thought, saying, what shall we eat? Or, what shall we drink? Or, wherewithal shall we be clothed? (For after all these things do the Gentiles seek) your heavenly Father knows that you have need of all these things." "But seek first the kingdom of Yahweh, and His righteousness, and all these things shall be added to you. Take no thought for the morrow. The morrow shall take thought for the things of itself. Sufficient to the day is the evil thereof."

"Judge not, that you be not judged. With what judgment you judge, you shall be judged. With what measure you mete, it shall be measured to you again. Why behold the mote that is in your brother's eye, but consider not the beam that is in your own eye? How will you say to your brother, let me pull out the mote out of your eye. And, behold, a beam is in your own eye?"

"You hypocrite, first cast out the beam out of your own eye, and then shall you see clearly to cast out the mote out of your brother's eye."

"Give not that which is holy to the dogs, neither cast your pearls before swine, lest they trample them under their feet, and turn again and rend you. Ask, and it shall be given you. Seek, and you shall find. Knock and it shall the opened to you. For everyone that asks will receive, and he that seeks will find, and to him that knocks it shall be opened."

"What man is there of you, whom if his son asks bread, will he give him a stone? If he asks a fish, will he give him a serpent? If you then, being evil, know to give good gifts to your children, how much more shall your Father which is heaven give good things to them that ask Him?"

"All things whatever you would that men should do to you, do so even to them. For this is the Law and the prophets. Enter in at the strait gate. For wide is the gate and broad is the way, that leads to destruction, and many there are which go in there. Strait is the gate, and narrow is the way, which leads to life, and few there are that find it."

"Beware of false prophets, which come to you in sheep's clothing, but inwardly they are ravening wolves. You shall know them by their fruits. Do men gather grapes of thorns or figs of thistles? Even so every good tree brings forth good fruit. But a corrupt tree brings forth evil fruit."

"A good tree cannot bring forth evil fruit, neither a corrupt tree bring forth good fruit. Every tree that brings not forth good fruit is hewn down, and cast into the fire. Wherefore by their fruits you shall know them."

"Not everyone that says to me, "Lord, Lord," shall enter into the kingdom of heaven. But only he that does the will of my Father who is in heaven will enter in."

"Many will say to me in that day, "Lord, Lord, have we not prophesied in Your Name? And in Your Name have cast out devils? And in Your Name done many wonderful works?" And then I will profess to them, "I never knew you. Depart from me you that work wickedness."

"Whoever hears these sayings of mine, and does them, I will liken him to a wise man, which built his house upon a rock. The rain descended, and the floods came, and the winds blew, and beat upon that house, and it fell not. For it was founded upon a rock.

Everyone that hears these sayings of mine and does them not, shall be likened to a foolish man, which built his house upon the sand. And the rain descended, and the floods came, and the winds blew, and beat upon that house, and it fell. And great was the fall of it."

It came to pass, when Yahshua had ended these sayings the people were astonished at His doctrine, for He taught them as one having authority, and not as the Scribes.

CHAPTER III

Yahshua came to Nazareth, where He had been brought up. As was His custom, He went into the synagogue on the Sabbath, and stood up to read. There was delivered to Him the book of the prophet Isaiah.

When He had opened the book, He found the place where it was written, "The Spirit of Yahweh is upon me because He has anointed me to preach the gospel to the poor. He has sent me to heal the broken-hearted, to preach deliverance to the captives, and recovering of sight to the blind, to set at liberty them that are bruised, to preach the acceptable year of Yahweh."

He closed the book, and gave it to the minister, and sat down. The eyes of all them that were in the synagogue were fastened on Him. He began to say unto them, "This day is this Scripture fulfilled in your ears." All bare Him witness and wondered at the gracious words which proceeded out of His mouth. And they said, "Is not this Joseph's son?" He said to them, "You will surely say to me this proverb, 'Physician heal yourself.

Whatever we have heard done in Capernaum do also here in your country.'"

He said, "Verily I say to you no prophet is accepted in his own country. But I tell you of a truth, many widows were in Israel in the days of Elijah, when the heaven was shut up three years and six months, when great famine was throughout all the land."

"Unto none of them was Elijah sent, save to Zarephath, of Sidon, to a woman, a widow. Many lepers were in Israel in the time of Elisha the prophet. None of them was cleansed, saving Naaman, the Syrian."

All they in the synagogue, when they heard these things were filled with wrath, and rose up, and thrust Him out of the city and led Him to the brow of the hill whereon their city was built, that they might cast Him down headlong. But He, passing through the midst of them, went His way down to Capernaum, He, His mother, His brothers, and His disciples.

On the Sabbath He entered into the synagogue and taught. They were astonished at His doctrine, for He taught them as one that had authority, and not as the Scribes.

There was in the synagogue a man with an unclean spirit, and he cried out, saying, "Let us alone. What have we to do with you, Yahshua of Nazareth? Have you come to destroy us? I know you, who you are, the Holy One of Yahweh." Yahshua rebuked him, saying, "Hold your peace, and come out of him." When the unclean spirit had torn him and cried with a loud voice, he came out of him, and hurt him not.

They were all amazed, insomuch that they questioned among themselves, saying, "What thing is this? What new doctrine is this? For with authority He commands even the unclean spirits, and they obey Him and come out." And immediately His fame spread abroad throughout the region about Galilee.

He arose out of the synagogue, and entered into Simon's house. Simon's wife's mother was taken with a great fever, and they besought Him for her. He stood over her, and rebuked the fever, and it left her, and immediately she arose and ministered unto them.

Now when the sun was setting, all they that had any sick with various diseases brought them unto Him, and He laid His hands on every one of them, and healed them. Devils also came out of many, crying out, and saying, "You are the Messiah, the Son of Yahweh." And He rebuking, suffered them not to speak, for they knew that He was the Messiah.

In the morning, rising up a great while before day, He went out, and departed into a solitary place, and there prayed. Simon and they that were with Him followed after Him, and when they had found Him, they said to Him, "All seek for you."

The people sought Him, and came to Him, and stayed Him that He should not depart from them. He said to them, "Let us go into the next towns, that I may preach the Kingdom of Yahweh to other cities as well, for therefore came I forth." He preached in the synagogues of Galilee, and cast out devils.

There came a leper to Him, beseeching Him, and kneeling down to Him, and saying to Him, "If you will, you can make me clean." Yahshua, moved with compassion, put forth His hand touched him, and said, "I will, be clean."

As soon as He had spoken the leprosy immediately departed from him, and he was cleansed. Yahshua strictly charged him, and forthwith sent him away saying, "See that you say nothing to any man, but go your way, show yourself to the priest, and offer for your cleaning those things which Moses commanded, as a testimony to them."

But he went out, and began to publish much, and to blaze abroad the matter, insomuch that Yahshua could no more openly enter into the city, but was without in desert places, and they came to Him from every quarter. So much the more went there fame abroad, and great multitudes came together to hear, and to be healed by Him of their infirmities. He withdrew Himself into the wilderness to pray.

It came to pass, that, as the people pressed upon Him to hear the Word of Yahweh; He stood by the Lake of Gennesaret, and saw two ships standing by the lake. But the fishermen were gone out of them, and were washing their nets. He entered into one of the ships, which was Simon's and prayed him that he would thrust out a little from the land. He then sat down, and taught the people out of the ship.

Great multitudes were gathered to Him, and He spoke many things to them in parables saying, "A sower went out to sow his seed, and as he sowed, some fell by the wayside, and it was trodden down, and the fowls of the air devoured them up."

"Some fell upon stony places where there was not much earth, and forthwith as soon as it was sprung up, because they had no deepness of earth, and when the sun was up they were scorched, and because it lacked moisture, and they had no root, they withered away. Some fell among thorns and the thorns sprang up with it, and choked them."

"Other seed fell into good ground, and brought forth fruit some a hundredfold, some sixtyfold, some thirtyfold. Who has ears to hear, let him hear."

The disciples came and said to Him, "Why do you speak unto them in parables?" He answered them, "Because it is given unto you to know the mysteries of the Kingdom of Heaven, but to them it is not given. Whoever has to him shall be given, and he shall have more abundance, but whoever has not, from him shall be taken away even that he has."

"I speak to them in parables, because seeing, they see not, and hearing, they hear not, neither do they understand. In them is fulfilled the prophecy of Isaiah which says, 'By hearing you shall hear and shall not understand, and seeing you shall see, and shall not perceive, for this people's heart is waxed gross and ears are dull of hearing, and they have closed their eyes, lest at any time they should see with eyes, and hear with ears, and should understand in their hearts and should be converted, and I should heal them.'"

"Blessed are your eyes, for they see, and your ears, for they hear. Verily I say to you, that many prophets and righteous have desired to see what you see, and have not, and to hear what you hear, and have not heard."

"Hear the parable of the sower, when anyone hears the Word of the Kingdom, and understands not, then comes the wicked one and catches away that which is sown in his heart. This is he which received seed by the wayside."

"He that receives seed into stony places, the same is he that hears the Word, and with joy receives it. Yet he has no root in himself, but endures for a while, but when tribulation or persecution arises because of the Word, by and by he is offended."

"He also that hears the Word among thorns is he that hears the Word and the cares of this world and he becomes unfruitful."

"But he that received seed into the good ground is he that hears the word, and understands, which also bears fruit, and brings forth, some a hundredfold, some sixty, and some thirty."

Another parable put Him forth to them saying, "The Kingdom of Heaven is like a man who sowed good seed in his field. While men slept, his enemy came and sowed tares among the wheat, and went his way."

"When the blade was sprung up, and brought forth fruit, then appeared the tares also. The servants of the householder came and said unto him, 'Sir, did you not sow good seed in your field? From whence then has it tares?' He said unto them, 'An enemy has done this.' The servants said unto him, 'Will you that we go and gather them up?'

But he said, 'Nay, lest while you gather up the tares, you root up also the wheat with them. Let both grow together until the harvest, and in the time of harvest I will say to the reapers, 'Gather together first the tares, and bind them in bundles to burn them, but gather the wheat into my barn.'"

Another parable He put to them saying, "The Kingdom of Heaven is like to a grain of mustard seed, which a man took and sowed in his field. Which indeed is the least of all seeds, but when it is grown it is the greatest among herbs, and becomes a tree, so that the birds of the air come and lodge in the branches thereof."

All these things spoke Yahshua to the multitudes in parables, and without a parable spoke He not unto them. That it might be fulfilled which was spoken by the prophet, saying, "I will utter things which have been kept secret from the foundation of the world."

Then Yahshua sent the multitude away, and went into the house, and His disciples came unto Him, saying, "Declare to us the parable of the tares of the field." He answered and said unto them, "He that sows the good seed is the Son of Man, the field is the world, the good seed are the children of the kingdom, but the tares are the children of the wicked. The enemy that sowed them is the devil. The harvest is the end of the world, and the reapers are the angels."

"As the tares are gathered and burned in the fire, so shall it be in the end of this world. The Son of Man shall send forth His angels and they shall gather out of His Kingdom all things that offend, and them that do iniquity, and shall cast them into a furnace of fire, there shall be wailing and gnashing of teeth."

"The righteous shall shine forth as the sun, in the kingdom of their Father. Who has ears to hear, let him hear. Again, the Kingdom of Heaven is like unto treasure hid in a field, which when a man has found, sells all that he has, and buys that field."

"Again, the Kingdom of Heaven is like unto a merchantman, seeking goodly pearls, who when he had found one pearl of great price, went and sold all that he had, and bought it."

"Again, the Kingdom of Heaven is like unto a net, that was cast into the sea, and gathered of every kind which, when it was full, they drew to shore, and sat down, and gathered the good into vessels, but cast the bad away."

"So shall it be at the end of the world, the angels shall come forth and sever the wicked from among the just, and shall cast them into the furnace of fire, there will be wailing and gnashing of teeth."

Yahshua said unto them, "Have you understood all these things?" They said to Him, "Yes Lord." He said to them, "Every scribe instructed in the Kingdom of Heaven is like a man who brings forth out of his treasure both new and old."

Yahshua said to them, "Is a candle brought to be placed under a bushel, or under a bed and not to be on a candlestick? For there is nothing hid, which shall not be manifested, neither was anything kept secret, but that it should come abroad."

Yahshua said to them, "Take heed what you hear, with what measure you mete it shall be measured to you, and unto you that hear shall more be given." He said, "So is the Kingdom of God, as if a man should cast seed into the ground, and should sleep, and rise night and day, and the seed should spring and grow up, he knows not how."

"The earth brings forth fruit of herself, first the blade, then the ear, after that the full corn in the ear. When the fruit is ripe he immediately puts in the sickle, because the harvest is come."

Now when He had left speaking, He said to Simon, "Launch out into the deep, and let down your nets for a drought." Simon answering said to Him, "Master, we have toiled all the night, and have taken nothing. Never the less at your word I will let down the net."

When he had done this, they enclosed a great multitude of fishes, and their net brake. They beckoned to their partners, who were in the other ship, that they should come and help them. They came and filled both ships so that they both began to sink.

When Simon Peter saw, he fell down at Yahshua' feet, saying, "Depart from me, for I am a sinful man, O Lord." He was astonished, and all that were with him at the drought of the fishes which they had taken.

So also were James and John, the sons of Zebedee, who were partners with Simon. Yahshua said to Simon, "Fear not, from henceforth you shall catch men." When they had brought their ships to land, they forsook all, and followed him.

When Yahshua entered Capernaum, there came to Him a Centurion, beseeching him, and saying, "Lord my servant lies at home sick of the palsy, grievously tormented." Yahshua said to him, "I will come and heal him."

The Centurion answered and said, "Lord I am not worthy that you should come under my roof, but speak the word only, and my servant shall be healed. For I am a man under authority, having soldiers under me and I say to this one, Go, and he goes, and to another Come, and he comes, and to my servant, Do this, and he does it."

When Yahshua heard, He marveled, and said to them that followed Him, "Verily I say to you, I have not found so great faith, no, not in Israel. Many shall come from the east and west, and shall sit down with Abraham and Isaac, and Jacob, in the Kingdom of Heaven, but the children of the kingdom shall be cast into outer darkness. There shall be weeping and gnashing of teeth." Yahshua said to the Centurion, "Go your way, and as you have believed so be it done to you." His servant was healed in the selfsame hour.

It came to pass on a certain day as he was teaching there were Pharisees and doctors of the law sitting by who came out of every town of Galilee, Judea, and Jerusalem, and the power of the Lord was to heal them. Behold, men brought in a bed a man who was taken with palsy, and they sought to bring him in and to lay him before Yahshua.

When they could not find by what way they might bring him in, because of the multitude, they went upon the housetop, and let him down through the tiling with the bed into the midst before Yahshua. When He saw their faith, He said to him, "Man, your sins are forgiven."

The Scribes and the Pharisees began to reason, saying "Who is this who speaks blasphemies? Who can forgive sins, but Yahweh alone?" When Yahshua perceived their thoughts, He answering said to them, "What reason you in your hearts? Which is easier to say, your sins are forgiven, or to say, rise up and walk?"

"That you may know that the Son of Man has power upon earth to forgive sins, (He said unto the sick of the palsy), I say to you, "Arise and take up your bed and go into your house."

Immediately he rose up before them, and took up that whereon he lay, and departed to his own house, glorifying Yahweh. They were all amazed, and they glorified Yahweh, and were filled with fear, saying, "We have seen strange things today."

After these things Yahshua went forth, and seeing a publican, named Levi, sitting at the receipt of custom, He said to him, "Follow me." Levi left all, rose up, and followed Yahshua. Levi made Him a great feast in his own house, and there was a great company of publicans and others that sat down with them.

The Scribes and Pharisees murmured against His disciples, saying, "Why do you eat and drink with publicans and sinners?" Yahshua answering said unto them, "They that are whole need not a physician, but they that are sick. I came not to call the righteous, but sinners to repentance."

Yahshua withdrew Himself with His disciples to the sea, and great multitudes from Galilee, Judea, Jerusalem, and Idumea and beyond Jordan, and they about Tyre and Sidon, a great multitude followed Him when they had heard what great things He did. He spoke to His disciples that a small ship should wait on Him because of the multitude, lest they should throng Him.

He had healed many, insomuch that they pressed upon Him for to touch Him, as many as had plagues. Unclean spirits, when, they saw Him, cried, saying, "You are the Son of Yahweh." He straightly charged them that they should not make Him known.

Now when Yahshua saw great multitudes about Him, He gave commandment to depart to the other side. A certain Scribe came and said to Him, "Master, I will follow you wherever you go."

Yahshua said to him, "The foxes have holes, and the birds of the air nests, but the Son of Man has nowhere to lay His head." Another of His disciples said to Him, "Lord, suffer me first to go and bury my father." Yahshua said to him, "Follow me, and let the dead bury their dead."

It came to pass when Yahshua entered into a ship with His disciples, He said to them, "Let us go over to the other side of the lake." As they sailed He fell asleep, and there arose a great tempest, a great storm of wind, and the waves beat into the ship so that it was now full.

Yahshua was in the hinder part of the ship, asleep on a pillow, and they woke Him, and said to Him, "Master, don't you care that we perish? Lord, save us." He said to them, "Why are you fearful, O you of little faith?"

He arose and rebuked the winds and the sea, and there was a great calm. He said to them, "How is it you have no faith?" And they feared exceedingly, and said one to another, "What manner of man is this, that even the wind and the sea obey Him?"

They came over to the other side of the sea, into the country of the Gadarenes. When He departed the ship there immediately met Him out of the tombs a man with an unclean spirit, who had been possessed with devils a long time.

He wore no clothes, neither abode in any house, but had dwelling among the tombs, and no man could bind him, no, not with chains, because he had been often bound with fetters and chains, and the chains had been plucked asunder by him, and the fetters broken in pieces. Neither could any tame him. And always, night and day, he was in the mountains, and in the tombs, crying, and cutting himself with stones.

When he saw Yahshua afar off, he ran and cried out, and fell down before Yahshua and with a loud voice said, "What have I to do with you Yahshua, Son of the Most High God? Have you come hither to torment us before the time? I adjure you by Yahweh, that you do not torment me."

Yahshua had commanded the unclean spirit to come out of the man, for oftentimes it had caught him, and he was kept bound with chains and fetters, and he broke the bands, and was driven of the devil into the wilderness.

Yahshua asked him, saying, "What is your name?" And he said, "Legion, for we are many." And they besought Him much that He would not send them away out of the country into the deep.

There was there a good way off from them a herd of many swine feeding on the mountain, and all the devils besought Him that He would suffer them to enter into them. He suffered them and forthwith Yahshua gave them leave to enter the swine.

The unclean spirits went out of the man, and entered into the swine, and the herd ran violently down a steep place into the sea (they were about two thousand), and were choked and perished in the sea.

They that fed the swine fled when they saw what had happened and went and told it in the city, and throughout the country. The whole city went out to see what had happened and came to Yahshua and found the man, out of whom the devils were cast, sitting at the feet of Yahshua, clothed and in his right mind, and they were afraid.

They that saw told how it befell him that was possessed with the devils, and with the swine.

They also which saw these things told them by what means he that was possessed of devils was healed. Then the whole multitude of the country of the Gadarenes round about besought Yahshua to depart from them, for they were taken with a great fear, and He went into the ship.

He that was possessed with the devils prayed Yahshua that he might go with Him. Howbeit Yahshua suffered him not, but said to him, "Return to your own house and to your friends, and tell them how great things Yahweh has done for you, and has shown compassion." He departed from them and began to publish in Decapolis how great things Yahshua had done for him, and all did marvel.

CHAPTER IV

When Yahshua had passed over again by ship to the other side, many people gathered about Him, and He was close to the sea. There came one of the rulers of the synagogues, Jairus by name, and when he saw Yahshua, he fell at His feet, and besought Him greatly, saying, "My little daughter lies at the point of death, come and lay hands on her, that she may be healed, and she shall live." He had only one daughter, about twelve years of age, and she lay dying. But as Yahshua went with him the people thronged Him.

A certain woman, who was diseased with an issue of blood for twelve years, had suffered many things of many physicians, and had spent all that she had, was nothing bettered, but rather grew worse, when she heard of Yahshua, came in the press behind and touched His garment. She said, "If I may but touch His clothes I shall be made whole." Straightway the fountain of her blood was dried up, and she felt in her body that she was healed of that plague.

Yahshua, immediately knowing that virtue had gone out of Him turned about in the press, and said, "Who touched my clothes?" The disciples said to Him, "You see the multitude thronging you, and you say, "Who touched me?" Yahshua said, "Somebody has touched me for I perceive that virtue is gone out of me." He looked about to see who had done this thing.

But the woman fearing and trembling, knowing what was done in her came and fell down before Him. She declared unto Him before all the people for what reason she had touched Him, and how she had been immediately healed. When Yahshua saw her, He said, "Daughter, be of good comfort, your faith has made you whole, go in peace, and be healed of the plague." And the woman was made whole from that hour.

While He yet spoke, there came one from the ruler of the synagogue's house, saying to him, "Your daughter is dead. Why do you trouble the Master any further?" When Yahshua heard, He answered saying, "Fear not, only believe and she shall be made whole." When He came into the house He suffered no man to follow Him save Peter, and James, and John, the brother of James, and the father and the mother of the maiden.

When He came into the house of the ruler of the synagogue, seeing the tumult, and them that wept and wailed greatly, He said unto them, "Why do you make this ado, and weep? The damsel is not dead, but sleeps." They laughed Him to scorn, knowing that she was dead.

When He had put them all out, He took the father and mother of the damsel, and them that were with Him, and entered in where the damsel was lying. He took the damsel by the hand, and said unto her, "Talithacumi" Which is being interpreted, "Damsel, (I say to you) arise." And her spirit came again, and she arose straightway and walked, for she was of twelve years of age. They were greatly astonished. Yahshua charged them strictly that no man should know it, and commanded that something should be given her to eat.

When Yahshua departed two blind men followed Him, crying, and saying, "Son of David, have mercy on us." When He came into the house, the two blind men came to Him, and saying to them, "Do you believe that I am able to do this?" They said to Him, "Yes Lord." He touched their eyes, saying, "According to your faith it is done to you." Their eyes were opened, and Yahshua strictly charged them saying, "See that no man know it." But they, when they had departed, spread abroad His fame throughout all that country.

As Yahshua departed, they brought to him a dumb man possessed with a devil. When the devil was cast out, the dumb spoke and the multitudes marveled, saying, "It has never been seen in Israel."

But the Pharisees said, "He casts out devils through the prince of devils".

    Yahshua went about all the cities and villages, teaching in their synagogues, and preaching the gospel of the kingdom, healing every sickness and every disease among the people. When He saw the multitudes He was moved with compassion on them, because they fainted, and were scattered abroad as sheep having no shepherd.

    Then said He to His disciples, the harvest truly is plenteous, but the laborers few, pray the Lord of the harvest, that He will send forth laborers into His harvest. And He went into a mountain to pray and called whom He would, and they came to Him.

    He ordained twelve, that they should be with Him, and that He might send them forth two by two to preach the Kingdom of God. He gave them power over unclean spirits to cast them out, to heal all manner of sickness and all manner of disease, and commanded them that they should take nothing for their journey, save a staff only, no script, no bread, no money in their purse, but shod only with sandals, and not to put on two coats."

    He said to them, "In whatever place you enter into a house, there abide until you depart from that place. Whoever shall not receive you, nor hear you, when you depart from there, shake off the dust under your feet for a testimony against them. Verily I say to you, it shall be more tolerable for Sodom and Gomorrah in the Day of Judgment than for that city."

They went through the towns preaching the Gospel that men should repent. They cast out many devils, anointed with oil many that were sick, and healed everywhere.

Now the names of the twelve apostles are these: The first Simon, who is called Peter, Andrew his brother, James of Zebedee, John, Philip, Bartholomew, Matthew the publican, Thomas, James the son of Alpheus, Thaddeus, Simon the Canaanite called Zelotes, and Judas Iscariot who was the traitor who betrayed Him.

These twelve Yahshua sent forth, and commanded them, saying, "Go not into the way of the Gentiles, and into any city of the Samaritans do not enter in but go rather to the lost sheep of the house of Israel."

"As you go preach saying, 'The Kingdom of Heaven is at hand.' Heal the sick, cleanse the lepers, raise the dead, cast out devils, freely you have received freely give. I send you forth as sheep in the midst of wolves, be therefore wise as serpents and harmless as doves."

"Beware of men for they will deliver you up to the councils, and they will scourge you in their synagogues, and you shall be brought before governors and kings for my sake, for a testimony against them and the Gentiles."

"When they deliver you up take no thought how or what you shall speak for it shall be given you in the same hour what you shall speak. It is not you that speaks, but the Spirit of your Father who speaks in you."

"The brother shall deliver up the brother to death, and the father the child, and the children shall rise up against their parents and cause them to be out to death. You shall be hated of all for my Name's sake, but he that endures to the end shall be saved."

"When they persecute you in this city, flee into another. Verily I say to you, "You shall not have gone over the cities of Israel till the Son of man is come. The disciple is not above his master, nor the servant above his lord. It is enough for the disciple that he is as his master, and the servant as his lord."

"If they have called the master of the house Beelzebub, how much more so will they call those of his household? It came to pass, when Yahshua had made an end of commanding His twelve disciples He departed from there to teach and to preach in their cities."

The Passover was at hand, and Yahshua went up to Jerusalem, and found in the Temple those that sold oxen and sheep and doves, and the changers of money sitting.

When He had made a scourge of small cords He drove them all out of the Temple, the sheep, and the oxen and poured out the changers' money, overthrew the tables, and said to them that sold doves, "Take these things hence make not my Father's house a house of merchandise."

His disciples remembered that it was written, "The zeal of your house has eaten me up." Then answered the rulers and said unto Him, "What sign do you show us, seeing that you do these things?" Yahshua answered and said to them, "Destroy this Temple, and in three days I will raise it up." The rulers said, "Forty-six years was this Temple in building and will you raise it up in three days?" But He spoke of the temple of His body.

When He had risen from the dead, His disciples remembered that He had said this to them, and they believed the Scripture, and the word which Yahshua had said.

There was a man of the Pharisees named Nicodemus, a ruler of the Jews, the same came to Yahshua by night, and said to Him, "Rabbi, we know that you are a teacher come from Yahweh, for no man does these miracles that you do except Yahweh be with Him."

Yahshua answered and said to him, "Verily, verily, I say to you, "Except a man be born again, he cannot see the Kingdom of Yahweh."

Nicodemus said to Him, "How can a man be born when he is old? Can he enter the second time into his mother's womb, and be born again?" Yahshua answered, "Verily, verily, I say to you, except a man be born of water and the Spirit, he cannot enter into the Kingdom of Yahweh."

"That which is born of flesh is flesh, and that which is born of the Spirit is spirit. Marvel not that I said to you, you must be born again. The wind blows where it lists, and you hear the sound of it, but cannot tell from where it comes, or where it goes, so is everyone that is born of the Spirit."

Nicodemus answered and said to Him, "How can these things be?" Yahshua answered and said to him, "Are you a master of Israel and you do not know these things? Verily, verily, I say to you, we speak that we do know, and testify that we have seen, and you receive not our witness. If I told you earthly things, and you don't believe, how shall you believe if I tell you heavenly things? No man has ascended up to heaven, but He that came down from heaven, the Son of Man which is in heaven."

"As Moses lifted up the serpent in the wilderness even so must the Son of Man be lifted up, that whoever believes in Him should not perish, but have eternal life. Yahweh so loved the world that He gave His only begotten Son, that whoever believes in Him shall not perish, but have everlasting life."

"Yahweh sent not His Son into the world to condemn the world, but that the world through Him might be saved. He that believes on Him is not condemned, but He that believes not is condemned already because he has not believed in the Name of the only begotten Son of Yahweh."

"This is the condemnation that light is come into the world, but men loved darkness rather than light, because their deeds were evil. Everyone that does evil hates the light neither comes to the light, lest his deeds should be reproved. But he that does truth comes to the light, that his deeds may be made manifest, that they are wrought in Yahweh."

When He was in Jerusalem at the Passover many believed in His Name when they saw the miracles which He did. But Yahshua did not commit Himself to them, because He knew all and needed not that any should testify of man for He knew what was in man.

After these things came Yahshua and His disciples into the land of Judea and there He tarried there with them and baptized the people. John was also baptizing in Aenon near to Salim, because there was much water there and they came and were baptized for John was not yet cast into prison.

There arose a question between John's disciples and the leaders about purifying. And they came to John, and said unto him, "Rabbi, He that was with you beyond Jordan, to whom you bare witness, the same baptizes, and all come to Him."

John answered and said, "A man can receive nothing, except it be given Him from heaven. You yourselves bear me witness, that. I said, I am not the Messiah, but that I am sent before Him. He that has the bride is the bridegroom, but the friend of the bridegroom, which stands and hears Him, rejoices greatly because of the bridegroom's voice."

"This is why my joy is fulfilled. He must increase, but I decrease. He that comes from above is above all he that is of the earth speaks of the earth. He that comes from above is above all. What He has seen and heard that He testifies, and no man receives His testimony. He that has received His testimony has set to His seal that Yahweh is true."

"He whom Yahweh has sent speaks the words of Yahweh, for Yahweh gives not the Spirit by measure. The Father loves the Son, and has given all things into His hand. He that believes on the Son has everlasting life, and he that believes not the Son shall not see life, but the wrath of Yahweh abides on him."

Herod the Tetrarch, being reproved by John for Herodias his brother Philip's wife, and for all the evils which Herod had done, added yet this above all, that he shut up John in prison. When John had heard in the prison, the works of the Messiah, he sent two of his disciples, and said to Him, "Are you He that should come, or do we look for another?"

Yahshua answered and said to them, "Go and show John those things which you hear and see, the blind receive their sight, the lame walk, the lepers are cleansed, the deaf hear, the dead are raised up, and the poor' have the gospel preached to them. And blessed is whoever shall not be offended in me."

As they departed Yahshua began to say to the multitudes concerning John, "What went you out into the wilderness to see, a reed shaken with the wind? What went you out to see, a man clothed in soft raiment? Behold, they that wear soft raiment are in kings houses. But what went you out to see, a prophet? Yes I say to you, and more than a prophet. This is he of whom it is written, 'Behold, I send My messenger before your face who shall prepare the way before you.'"

"Verily I say to you, among them that are born of women there has not risen a greater than John the Baptist, notwithstanding, he that is least in the Kingdom of Heaven is greater than he. From the days of John the Baptist until now the Kingdom of Heaven suffers violence, and the violent take it by force. For all the prophets and the law prophesied until John. If you will receive it, this is Elijah, who was to come." He that has ears to hear, let him hear."

"Where to shall I liken this generation? It is like children sitting in the markets, and calling unto their fellows, and saying, 'We have piped to you, and you have not danced, we have mourned for you, and you have not lamented.'"

"John came neither eating nor drinking, and they say, he has a devil. The Son of man came eating and drinking, and they say, 'Behold a man gluttonous, and a winebibber, a friend of publicans and sinners.' But wisdom is justified of her children".

When the Lord knew how the Pharisees had heard that Yahshua made and baptized more than John, (though Yahshua Himself baptized not, but His disciples.) He left Judea and departed again into Galilee. He must go through Samaria. He came to a city of Samaria, which is called Sychar, near to the parcel of ground whereon was Jacob's well. Yahshua, being wearied with journey set on the well, it was about the sixth hour.

There came a woman of Samaria to draw water. Yahshua said to her, "Give me to drink." The woman of Samaria said to Him, "How is it that you, being a Jew, ask drink of me who is a woman of Samaria? For the Jews have no dealings with the Samaritans."

Yahshua answered and said to her, "If you knew the gift of Yahweh, and who it is that said to you, 'Give me to drink,' you would have asked Him, and He would have given you living water."

The woman said unto Him, "Sir, you have nothing to draw with, and the well is deep, from where then have you that living water? Are you greater than our father Jacob, who gave us the well, and drank thereof himself, and his children, and his cattle?"

Yahshua answered and said to her, "Whoever drinks of this water shall thirst again, but whoever drinks of the water that I shall give him shall never thirst. The water that I shall give him shall be in him a well of water springing up into everlasting life."

The woman said to him, "Sir, give me this water, that I thirst not, neither come hither to draw." Yahshua said unto her, "Go, call your husband, and come here." The woman answered and said, "I have no husband." Yahshua said to her, "You have spoken well, 'I have no husband,' for you have had five husbands, and he whom you have is not your husband. In that you have spoken truly."

The woman said to Him, "Sir, I perceive that you are a prophet. Our fathers worshipped in this mountain, and you say, that in Jerusalem is the place where men ought to worship." Yahshua said to her, "Woman, believe me, the hour comes, when you shall neither in this mountain, nor yet at Jerusalem, worship the Father. You worship you know not what we know what we worship, for salvation is of the Jews."

"But the hour comes, and now is, when true worshipers shall worship the Father in spirit and in truth. For the Father seeks such to worship Him. Yahweh is a Spirit, and they that worship Him must worship in spirit and in truth." The woman said to Him, "I know that Messiah comes. When He is come, He will tell us all things." Yahshua said to her, "I that speak to you am he."

Upon this came His disciples, and marveled that He talked with the woman, yet no man said, "What do you seek?" Or, "Why do you talk with her? " The woman then left her water pot, and went into the city, and said to the men, "Come, see a man, who told me all things that ever I did. Is this not the Messiah?" Then they went out of the city, and came to Him.

Meanwhile His disciples prayed Him, saying, "Master, eat." He said to them, "I have meat to eat that you know not of." The disciples said to one another, "Has any man brought Him something to eat?" Yahshua said to them, "My meat is to do the will of Him that sent me, and to finish His work. Say not there are yet four months, and comes the harvest? Behold, I say to you, "Lift up your eyes, and look on the fields, for they are white already to harvest."

"He that reaps receives wages, and gathers fruit unto life eternal, that both he that sows and he that reaps may rejoice together. Herein is that saying true one sows and another reaps. I send you to reap that whereupon you bestowed no labor, other men labored, and you have entered into their labors."

Many Samaritans of that city believed on Him for the saying of the woman, which testified, "He told me all that ever I did." So when the Samaritans came to Him, they besought Him that He would stay with them, and He abode there two days. Many more believed because of His word, and they said to the woman, "Now we believe, not because of your saying, for we have heard ourselves, and know that this is indeed the Messiah, the Savior of the world."

After two days He departed from there and went into Galilee. Yahshua Himself testified that a prophet has no honor in his own country. When He had come to Galilee, the Galileans received Him, having seen all the things that He did at Jerusalem at the feast, for they also went to the feast.

Yahshua came again into Cana of Galilee where He turned the water into wine. There was a certain nobleman, whose son was sick at Capernaum. When he heard that Yahshua had come out of Judea into Galilee, he went to Him, and besought Him that He would come down and heal his son, for he was at the point of death. Yahshua said to him, "Except you see signs and wonders, you will not believe." The nobleman said to Him, "Sir, come down or my child will die."

Yahshua said to him, "Go your way, your son lives." And the man believed the word that

Yahshua had spoken to him, and he went his way. As he was now going down, his servants met him, and said, "Your son lives." He inquired of them the hour when he began to mend. They said to him, "Yesterday at the seventh hour the fever left him."

So the father knew that at the same hour in which Yahshua said to him, "Your son lives." He believed, and his whole house. This is again the second miracle Yahshua did when He came out of Judea into Galilee.

CHAPTER V

At that time Herod the Tetrarch heard of all that was done by Yahshua and he was perplexed, because it was said of some, that John was risen from the dead, and of some, that Elijah had appeared, and of others, that one of the old prophets was risen again.

Herod said, "John have I beheaded, but who is this of whom I hear such things?" And he desired to see Yahshua. For Herod himself had sent forth and laid hold upon John, and bound him in prison for Herodias' sake, his brother Philip's wife, for he had married her. John had said unto Herod, "It is unlawful for you to have your brother's wife."

Herodias had a quarrel against John and would have killed him, but she could not. For Herod feared John and the multitudes, knowing that he was a just man and a holy, and observed him, and when he heard him, he did many things, and heard him gladly.

When a convenient day had come, Herod on his birthday made a supper for his lords, high captains, and chiefs of Galileo, and when the daughter of Herodias came in and danced, it pleased Herod and them that sat with him. The king said to the damsel, "Ask of me whatever you will, and I will give it to you." And he swore to her, "Whatever you shall ask of me, I will give it to you, to the half of my kingdom."

She went forth and said to her mother, "What shall I ask?" And she said, "The head of John the Baptist." And she came straightway with haste to the king, and asked, saying, "I will that you give me by and by in a charger the head of John the Baptist." The king was exceedingly sorry, for his oath's sake, and for their sakes which sat with him, he would not reject her.

Immediately the king sent an executioner, and commanded that John's head be brought. He went and beheaded John in prison, and brought his head in a charger and gave it to the damsel and the damsel gave it to her mother. When his disciples heard of it, they came and took up the corpse, and laid it in a tomb.

When Yahshua heard, He departed from there by ship into a desert place apart. The apostles gathered themselves together to Yahshua, and told Him all things, both what they had done, and what they had taught. He said to them, "Come apart and rest awhile." For there were many coming and going and they had no leisure so much as to eat.

The people saw them departing, and many knew Him and ran afoot out of all cities and out went them, and came together to Him. Yahshua, when He came out, saw a great multitude, and was moved with compassion toward them, because they were as sheep not having a shepherd. And He began to teach them many things, and He healed their sick.

When the day was now far spent, and it was evening, His disciples came to Him, saying, "This is a desert place, and now the time is far passed, send the multitude away that they may go into the country round about, and into the villages, and buy themselves bread, for they have nothing to eat." He said to Philip, "Where shall we buy bread that these may eat?"

This He said to prove him, for He Himself knew what He would do. Philip answered Him, "Two Hundred pennyworth of bread is not sufficient that every one of them may take a little." One of His disciples, Andrew, Simon Peter's brother, said to him, "There is a lad here, who has five barley loaves, and two small fish, but what are they among so many?"

Yahshua commanded them to make everyone sit down by companies on the green grass. They sat down in ranks, by hundreds, and by fifties. When He had taken the five loaves and the two fish,

He looked up to heaven, and blessed and broke the loaves, and gave to His disciples to set before them, and the two fish He divided among them all. And they ate and were filled. They that had eaten were about five thousand men, beside women and children.

When they were filled, He said to His disciples." Gather up the fragments that remain, that nothing be lost." They gathered together, and filled twelve baskets with fragments of the five barley loaves, which remained over and above to them that had eaten.

Then those men, they had seen the miracle that Yahshua did, said, "This is of a truth that prophet that should come into the world." When Yahshua perceived that they would come and take Him by force, to make Him a king, He constrained His disciples to get into a ship, and to go before Him to the other side unto Bethsaida, while He sent the multitudes away.

When He had sent the people away, He went up into a mountain apart to pray. When evening had come He was there alone. But the ship was now in the midst of the sea, tossed with waves, for the wind was contrary. In the fourth watch of the night Yahshua went to them, walking on the sea, and would have passed them by, but when they saw Him walking upon the sea, they supposed it had been a spirit, and cried out for fear, for they all saw Him and were troubled. Immediately He talked with them, and said to them, "Be of good cheer, it is I, be not afraid."

Peter answered Him and said, "Lord, if it be you, bid me come to you on the water." He said, "Come." When Peter came down out of the ship, he walked on the water, to go to Yahshua. And when he saw the wind boisterous, he was afraid, and beginning to sink, he cried, saying, "Lord, save me." Immediately Yahshua stretched forth His hand, and caught him, and said to him, "O man of little faith, why did you doubt?"

When they came into the ship, the wind ceased. They that were in the ship came and worshipped Him, saying, "Of a truth you are the Son of God." and they were sore amazed in themselves beyond measure, and wondered. They considered not the loaves, for their hearts were hardened.

When they had crossed over, they came into the land of Gennesaret. And when the men of that place had knowledge of Him, they sent out into all that country round about, and brought to Him all that were diseased, and besought Him that they might only touch the hem of His garment, and as many as touched were made perfectly whole.

The day following, when the people which stood on the other side of the sea, saw that there was none other boat there, save that one where into His disciples had entered, and that Yahshua went not with His disciples into the boat, but His disciples had gone away alone. (Howbeit, there came other boats from Tiberius close to the place where they ate bread, after the Lord had given thanks). When the people saw that Yahshua was not there, nor His disciples, they also took shipping, and came to Capernaum, seeking Yahshua.

When they found Him on the other side of the sea, they said to Him, "Rabbi, when did you come here?" Yahshua answered them and said, "Verily, verily, I say to you, you seek me, not because you saw the miracles, but because you did eat of the loaves, and were filled. Do not labor for the meat that perishes but labor for that meat which endures to everlasting life, which only the Son of Man shall give you. For He alone has Yahweh, the Father, sealed.

Then said they to Him, "What shall we do, that we might work the works of Yahweh?" Yahshua answered and said to them, "This is the work of Yahweh that you believe on Him whom He has sent."

They said to Him, "What sign do you show then, that we may see and believe you? What do you work? Our fathers did eat manna in the desert, as it is written Yahweh gave them bread from heaven to eat."

Yahshua said to them, "Verily, verily, I say to you, Moses gave you not that bread from heaven, but my Father gives you the true bread from heaven. The bread of Yahweh is He who comes down from heaven, and gives life to the world." He said to them, "I am the bread of life. He that comes to me shall never hunger, and he that believes on me shall never thirst. But I said to you, that you also have seen me, and believe not."

"All that the Father gives me shall come to me, and him that comes to me I will in no wise cast out. I came down from heaven, not to do my own will, but the will of Him that sent me. This is my Father's will which has sent me, that of all which He has given me I should lose nothing, but should raise it up again at the last day, and this is the will of Him that sent me, that everyone who sees the Son, and believes on Him, may have everlasting life, and I will raise him up at the last day."

The rulers then murmured at Him because He said, "I am the bread which came down from heaven." And they said, "Is not this Yahshua, the son of Yosef, whose father and mother we know?"

"How is it then that He said, "I came down from heaven?" Yahshua answered and said to them, "Murmur not amongst yourselves. No man can come to me, except the Father which has sent me draw him, and I will raise him up at the last day. It is written in the prophets, 'They shall all be taught of Yahweh.' Every man that has heard, and has learned of the Father, comes to me."

"Not that any man has seen the Father, save He who is of Yahweh He has seen the Father. Verily, verily, I say to you, he that believes on me has everlasting life. I am that bread of life. Your fathers did eat manna in the wilderness, and are dead. This is the bread which comes down from heaven, that many may eat thereof, and not die. I am the living bread which came down from heaven, if any man eats of this bread he shall live forever, and the bread that I will give is my flesh, which I will give for the life of the world."

The rulers therefore strove among themselves, saying, "How can this man give us flesh to eat?" Yahshua said to them, "Verily, I say to you, 'Except you eat the flash of the Son of Man, and drink His blood, you have no life in you.' Whoever eats my flesh, and drinks my blood, has eternal life, and I will raise him up at the last day."

"My flesh is meat indeed, and my blood is drink indeed. He that eats my flesh, and drinks my blood, dwells in me, and I in him. As the living Father has sent me, and I live by the Father, so he that eats me, even he shall live by me. This is that bread which came down from heaven, not as your fathers did eat manna, and are dead. He that eats of this bread shall live forever." These things He said in the synagogue, as He taught in Capernaum.

Many of His disciples, when they had heard, said, "This is a hard saying, who can hear it?" When Yahshua knew in Himself that His disciples murmured at it, He said to them, "Does this offend you? If you shall see the Son of Man ascend up where He was before? It is the Spirit that quickens, the flesh profits nothing."

"The words that I speak to you are Spirit and they are life. There are some of you that believe not." Yahshua knew from the beginning who believed not, and who should betray Him. He said, "Therefore said I to you that no man can come to me, except it was given to him of my Father."

From that time many of His disciples went back, and walked no more with Him. Then Yahshua said to the twelve, "Will you also go away?" Simon Peter answered Him, "Lord, to whom we shall go? You have the words of eternal life. We believe and are sure that you are the Messiah, the Son of the living God." Yahshua answered them, "Have I not chosen you twelve, and one of you is a devil?" He spoke of Judas Iscariot the son of Simon, for he it was that should betray Him, being one of the twelve.

One of the Pharisees desired Him that He would eat with him. He went into the Pharisee's house, and sat down to meat. And behold, a woman in the city, which was a sinner, when she knew that Yahshua sat at meat in the Pharisee's house, brought an alabaster box of ointment, and stood at His feet behind weeping and began to wash His feet with tears, and did wipe with the hairs of her head, and kissed His feet, and anointed them with the ointment.

When the Pharisee who had invited Him saw this, he spoke within himself, saying, "This man, if He were a prophet, would have known who and what manner of woman that touches Him, for she is a sinner."

Yahshua, answering said to him, "Simon, I have somewhat to say to you." And he said, "Master, say on." "There was a certain creditor which had two debtors, the one owed five hundred pence, and the other fifty. And when they had nothing to pay, he frankly forgave them both. Tell be therefore, which of them will love him most?" Simon answered and said, "I suppose that to whom he forgave most." And He said unto him, "You have rightly judged."

Yahshua turned to the woman, and said to Simon, "Do you see this woman? I entered into your house, you gave me no water for my feet, but she has washed my feet with tears, and wiped them with the hairs of her head. You gave me no kiss, but this woman, since the time I came in, has not ceased to kiss my feet. My head with oil you did not anoint, but this woman has anointed my feet with ointment. Wherefore, I say to you, 'Her sins, which are many, are forgiven, for she loved much, but to whom little is forgiven, loves little."

He said to her, "Your sins are forgiven." They that sat at meat with Him began to say within themselves, "Who is this that forgives sins also?" He said to the woman, "Your faith has saved you, go in peace."

It came to pass afterward, that He went throughout every city and village, preaching and showing the glad tidings of the Kingdom of Yahweh, and the twelve with Him, and certain women, who had been healed of evil spirits and infirmities, Mary called Magdalene, out of whom went seven devils, and Joanna the wife of Chuza, Herod's steward, and Susanna, and many others, who ministered to Him of their substance.

Then Yahweh went from there, and departed into the coasts of Tyre and Sidon, and entered into a house and would have no man know it. But He could not be hid. A woman of Canaan, whose young daughter had an unclean spirit, heard of Him, and came and fell at His feet, and cried unto Him, saying, "Have mercy on me, O Lord, Son of David, my daughter is grievously vexed with a devil."

He answered her not a word, for she was a Greek, a Syrophoenician by nation, and she besought Him that He would cast forth the devil out of her daughter.

His disciples came and besought Him, saying, "Send her away, for she cries after us." But He answered and said, "I am not sent but to the lost sheep of the house of Israel." Then she came and worshipped Him, saying, "Lord, help me." Yahshua said to her, "Let the children first be filled, for it is not meet to take the children's bread, and to cast it to the dogs." She answered and said to Him, "Yes, Lord, yet the dogs under the table eat of the children's crumbs."

Then Yahshua answered and said to her, "O woman great is your faith, for this saying go your way, be it done to you even as you will, the devil is gone out of your daughter." Her daughter was made whole from that very hour. When she came to her house, she found the devil gone out, and her daughter laid upon the bed.

And again, departing from the coasts of Tyre and Sidon, Yahshua came to the Sea of Galilee through the midst of the coasts of Decapolis. They brought to Him one that was deaf, and had an impediment in his speech, and they pleaded with Him to put His hand upon him.

Yahshua took him aside from the multitude, and put His fingers into his ears, and He spit, and touched his tongue and looking up to heaven, He sighed, and said unto him,"Ephphatha," that is, "Be opened." And straightway his ears were opened, and the string of his tongue was loosed, and he spoke plain.

Yahshua charged them that they should tell no man. But the more He charged them, so much the more a great deal they published, and were beyond measure astonished, saying, "He has done all things well, He makes both the deaf to hear, and the dumb to speak, the blind to see," and they glorified Yahweh, the God of Israel.

In those days the multitude being very great, and having nothing to eat, Yahshua called His disciples, and said to them, "I have compassion on the multitude, because they continue with me now three days, and have nothing to eat, and I will not send them away fasting, lest they faint in the way, for divers of them have come from afar." His disciples answered Him, "Where should we have so much bread in the wilderness, as to fill so great a multitude?"

Yahshua asked them, "How many loaves have you?" They answered and said, "Seven and a few fishes." He commanded the people to sit on the ground, and He took the seven loaves, gave thanks, broke the bread, and gave to His disciples to set before the people. They also had a few small fish which He blessed and commanded them to set these also before the people.

So they did eat, and were filled, and they took up of the broken bread that was left seven baskets full. They that had eaten were about four thousand men, besides women and children. And He sent away the multitude and took ship with His disciples, and came to the parts of Dalmanutha, and into the coast of Magdala.

The Pharisees, also with the Sadducees, came and tempting desired Him that He would show them a sign from heaven. He answered and said to them, "When it is evening, you say fair weather, for the sky is red, and in the morning, foul weather today, for the sky is red and lowering. O hypocrites, you can discern the face of the sky, but can you not discern the signs of the times? A wicked and adulterous generation seeks after a sign, and there shall no sign be given it, but the sign of the prophet Jonah."

"As Jonah was a sign to the Ninevites, so also shall the Son of Man be to this generation. The queen of the south shall rise up in judgment with this generation, and shall condemn it, for she came from the uttermost parts of the earth to hear the wisdom of Solomon, and, behold, a greater than Solomon is here."

Yahshua said to the people, "When you see a cloud rise out of the west, straightway you say, 'There comes a shower', and so it is. When the South winds blow, you say, 'There will be heat', and it comes to pass. Hypocrites, you can discern the face of the sky and of the earth. But how is it that you do not discern this time?"

Yahshua left them, and entering into the ship again departed to the other side. Having forgotten to take bread neither had they more than one loaf in the ship with them. He charged them, saying, "Take heed, and beware of the leaven of the Pharisees, and of the Sadducees."

They reasoned among themselves, saying, "Because we have taken no bread." When Yahshua perceived, He said to them, "Why do you reason because you have no bread? Do you not perceive nor understand? Have you your hearts yet hardened having eyes you see not? Having ears, hear you not? Don't you remember?"

"When I broke the five loaves among the five thousand, how many baskets full of fragments did you take up?" They said to Him, "Twelve." "And the seven loaves among four thousand, how many baskets full of fragments did you take up?" And they said, "Seven."

"How is it that you do not understand that I spoke not to you concerning bread, but that you should beware of the leaven of the Pharisees and of the Sadducees?" Then they understood how He bade them not to beware of the leaven of bread, but of the doctrine of the Pharisees and of the Sadducees.

He came to Bethsaida, and they brought a blind man to Him, and besought Him to touch him. He took the blind man by the hand, and led him out of the town, and when He had spit on his eyes, and put His hands upon him, He asked him if he saw clearly. He looked up and said, "I see men as trees walking."

After that He put hands again upon the blind man's eyes, and made him look up, and he was restored, and saw every man clearly. Yahshua sent him away to his house, saying, "Neither go into the town, nor tell to any in the town."

Yahshua was teaching in one of the synagogues on the Sabbath. There was a woman who had a spirit of infirmity eighteen years, and was bound together, and could in no wise lift herself up. When Yahshua saw her, He called and said to her, "Woman, you are loosed from your infirmity." He laid hands on her, and immediately she was made straight, and glorified Yahweh.

The ruler of the synagogue answered with indignation, because Yahshua had healed on the Sabbath, and said to the people, "There are six days in which men ought to work, in them therefore come and be healed, but not on the Sabbath."

Yahshua answered him, and said, "Hypocrite does not each one of you on the Sabbath loose his ox or his ass from the stall, and lead him away to watering? Should not this woman, being a daughter of Abraham, whom Satan has bound, lo, these eighteen years, is loosed from this bond on the Sabbath?"

When He had said these things, all His adversaries were ashamed, and all the people rejoiced for all the glorious things that were done by Him.

CHAPTER VI

After these things Yahshua appointed another seventy also, and sent them two by two before His face into every city and place whither He Himself would come. Yahshua said to them, "The harvest truly is great, but the laborers are few, pray the Lord of the harvest, that He would send forth laborers into His harvest."

"Go your way, behold I send you forth as lambs among wolves. Carry neither purse, nor scrip, nor shoes, and salute no man by the way. Into whatever house you enter, first say, 'Peace to this house.'"

"If the son of peace is there, your peace shall rest upon it, if not, it shall turn to you again. In the same house remain, eating and drinking such things as they give, for the laborer is worthy of his hire. Go not from house to house. Into whatever city you enter, and they receive you, eat such things as are set before you."

"Heal the sick that are therein, and say to them, the Kingdom of God is come nigh unto you. Into whatever city you enter, and they receive you not, go your way out into the streets of the same, and say, 'Even the very dust of your city, which cleaves on us we do wipe off against you' notwithstanding, be sure of this, that the Kingdom of Yahweh is come close to you.'"

"I say to you, that it shall be more tolerable in that day for Sodom, than for that city. Woe to you Corazin! Woe to you Bethsaida! For if the mighty works had been done in Tyre and Sidon which have been done in you, they had a great while ago repented, sitting in sackcloth and ashes."

"It shall be more tolerable for Tyre and Sidon at the judgment, than for you. And Capernaum, which is exalted to heaven, shalt be thrust down to hell. He that hears you hears me, and he that despises you despises me, and he that despises me despises Him that sent me."

The seventy returned again with joy saying, "Lord, even the devils are subject to us through your Name." He said to them, "I beheld Satan as lightning fall from heaven."

"I give you power to tread on serpents and scorpions, and over all the power of the enemy and nothing shall by any means hurt you."

"Notwithstanding, in this rejoice not that the spirits are subject to you, but rather rejoice because your names are written in heaven."

In that hour Yahshua rejoiced in Spirit, and said, "I thank You, Father, Lord of heaven and earth, that You have hid these things from the wise and the prudent and has revealed them to babes, even so Father, for so it seemed good in Your sight."

"All things are delivered to me of my Father, and no man knows who the Son is, but the Father, and who the Father is, but the Son, and to whom the Son will reveal it".

He turned to the disciples, and said privately, "Blessed are the eyes which see the things that you see, for I tell you that many prophets and kings have desired to see those things which you see, and have not seen, and to hear those things which you hear, and have not heard."

A certain lawyer stood up, and tempted Him, saying, "Master, what shall I do to inherit eternal life?" Yahshua asked him, "What is written in the law? How do you read it?" He answering said, "You shall love the Lord your God with all your heart, and with all your soul, with all your strength, and with your entire mind, and your neighbor as yourself." Yahshua said to him, "You have answered right. Do this and you shall live."

But he, willing to justify himself, said to Yahshua, "And who is my neighbor?" Yahshua answering said, "A certain man went down from Jerusalem to Jericho, and fell among thieves, who stripped him of his raiment, wounded him, and departed, leaving him half dead."

"By chance there came down a certain priest that way, and when he saw him, he passed by on the other side. Likewise a Levite, when he was at the place, came and looked, and passed by on the other side."

"But a certain Samaritan, as he journeyed, came where he was, and when he saw him, he had compassion, and went and bound up his wounds, pouring in oil and wine, and set him on his own beast, and brought him to an inn, and took care of him."

"On the morrow when he departed, he took out two pence, and gave it to the host, and said to him 'take care of him, and whatever you spend more, when I come again, I will repay you.'"

"Which now of these three do you think was a neighbor to him that fell among thieves?" And he said, "He that showed mercy on him." Then Yahshua said to him, "Go, and do likewise."

It came to pass, as Yahshua was praying, His disciples were with Him, and He asked them saying, "Who do the people say that I am?" They answered Him and said, "John the Baptist, some Elijah, and others, that one of the old prophets have risen again."

He said to them, "But who do you say that I am?" Peter answering said, "You are the Messiah the Son of the living God." Yahshua answered and said to him, "Blessed are you, Simon Bar-Jonas, for flesh and blood has not revealed this to you, but my Father who is in heaven. I say also to you, that you are Peter, and upon this rock, (referring to the statement that He is the Son of Yahweh), I will build my church, and the gates of hell shall not prevail against it. I will give to you the keys of the Kingdom of Heaven, and whatever you shall loose on earth shall be loosed in Heaven."

He strictly charged His disciples and commanded to tell no man the thing, saying, "The Son of Man must suffer many things, and be rejected of the Elders and Chief Priests and Scribes, and be slain, and be raised the third day."

Yahshua said to all, "If any will come after me, let him deny himself and die daily and follow me. Whoever will save his life shall lose it, but whoever will lose his life for my sake, the same shall save it."

"What is a man advantaged, if he gains the whole world, and loses himself, or be cast away? For whoever shall be ashamed of me and of my words, of him shall the Son of Man be ashamed when He shall come in the glory of His Father and with the holy angels, and then He shall reward every man according to his works. I tell you of a truth, there are some standing here, who shall not taste of death till they see the Kingdom of God."

Now the Feast of Tabernacles was at hand. His brethren said to Yahshua, "Depart from here and go into Judea, that your disciples also may see the works that you do. For no man does anything in secret, and he himself seeks to be known openly. If you do these things, show yourself to the world." For none of His brethren believed in Him.

Yahshua said to them, "My time has not yet come, but your time is always ready. The world cannot hate you, but me it hates, because I testify of it that the works thereof are evil. You go to this Feast, for my time is not yet fully come." When He had said these words unto them, He continued his abode in Galilee. When His brethren were gone on, then He also went up to the Feast, not openly, but as it were, in secret.

The Chief Priests sought him at the Feast saying, "Where is He?" There was much discussion among the people concerning Him, for some said,

"He is a good man." Others said, "Nay, He deceives the people. But no man spoke openly about Him for fear of the Chief Priests.

Now about the midst of the Feast of Tabernacles Yahshua went into the Temple and taught. And the Chief Priests marveled, saying, "How does this man know letters, having never learned?"

Yahshua answered them, and said, "My doctrine is not mine, but His that sent me. If any man will do His will, He shall know of the doctrine, whether it is of Yahweh, or if I speak of myself."

"He that speaks of himself seeks his own glory, but He that seeks His glory that sent Him, the same is true, and no unrighteousness is in Him. Did not Moses give you the law, and none of you keeps the law? Why do you go about seeking to kill me?"

The Chief Priests answered and said, "You have a devil, who goes about to kill you?" Yahshua answered and said to them, "I have done one work, and you all marvel. Moses gave you circumcision, (not because it is of Moses, but of the fathers), and you on the Sabbath circumcise a man."

"If a man on the Sabbath shall receive circumcision, that the Law of Moses should not be broken, are you angry with me, because I have made a man every whit whole on the Sabbath? Judge not according to the appearance, but judge righteous judgment"

Then said some of them of Jerusalem, "Is not this He whom they seek no kill? But, lo, He speaks boldly, and they say nothing to Him. Do the rulers know indeed that this is the very Messiah? Howbeit we know this man whence He is, but when Messiah comes, no man knows whence He is."

Then cried Yahshua in the Temple as He taught saying, "You both know me, and you know whence I am, and I have not come of myself, but He that sent me is true, whom you do not know. But I know Him, for I am from Him, and He has sent me."

Then they sought to take Him, but no man laid hands on Him because His hour had not yet come. Many people believed on Him, and said, "When the Messiah comes will He do more miracles than these which this man has done?"

The Pharisees and the Chief Priests sent officers to take Him. Then said Yahshua to them, "Yet a little while I am with you I go to Him that sent me. You will seek me, and you will not find me, and where I am, you cannot come."

Then said the rulers among themselves, "Where will He go that we shall not find him? Will

He go to the dispersed among the Gentiles, and teach the Gentiles? What saying is this that He has said, 'You shall seek me, and shall not find me,' and, 'Where I am you cannot come?'

On the last day, that great (day) of the Feast of Tabernacles, Yahshua stood and cried, "If any man thirst let him come to me and drink, He that believes on me, as the Scriptures have said, 'Out of his belly shall flow rivers of living water.'"

(But this spoke He of the Spirit, which they that believe on Him should receive, for the Holy Spirit had not yet been given, because Yahshua was not yet glorified).

Many of the people when they heard this saying, said, "Of a truth this is the prophet." Others said, "This is the Messiah." But some said, "Shall the Messiah come out of Galilee? Has not the Scripture said that the Messiah comes of the seed of David and out of the town of Bethlehem where David was?" So there was a division among the people because of Him.

Then came the officers to the Chief Priests and Pharisees, and they said to them, "Why have you not bought Him?" The officers answered, "Never has any man spoken like this man." The Pharisees answered them, "Are you also deceived?

Have any of the rulers believed on Him? But this people who know not the law are cursed."

Nicodemus said to them, (this was he that came to Yahshua by night being one of them), "Does our law judge any man, before it hear him, and know what he does?" They answered and said unto him, "Are you also of Galilee? Search, and look, for out of Galilee arises no prophet." And every man went to his own home.

Yahshua went to the Mount of Olives. Early in the morning He came again into the Temple, and all the people came to Him, and He sat down, and taught them.

The Scribes and Pharisees brought to Him a woman taken in adultery, and when they had set her in the midst, they said to Him, "Master, this woman was taken in adultery, in the very act. Now Moses in the Law commanded us, that such should be stoned, but what do you say?"

This they said tempting Him, that they might have something to accuse Him of. But Yahshua stooped down, and with finger wrote on the ground.

When they continued asking Him, He lifted Himself up and said to them, "He that is without sin among you, let him first cast a stone at her." Again He stopped down, and wrote on the ground.

They, who heard, being convicted by their own conscience, went out one by one, beginning with the eldest to the least. Yahshua was left with the woman standing in the midst of them.

When Yahshua had lifted Himself up and saw none but the woman, He said to her, "Woman, where are those who have accused you? Has no one condemned you?" She said, "No man, Lord." Yahshua said to her, "Neither do I condemn you, go, and sin no more."

Than Yahshua spoke again to them, saying, "I am the light of the world. He that follows me shall not walk in darkness, but shall have the light of life."

The Pharisees to Him, "You bear record of yourself. Your record is not true." Yahshua answered and said to them, "Though I bear record of myself my record is true. For I know from where I came, and whither I go, but you cannot tell where I come from, and whither I go. You judge after the flesh, I judge no man. And yet if I judge, my judgment is true, for I am not alone, but I and the Father that sent me."

"It is written in your law that the testimony of two men is true. I am one that bears witness of myself and the Father also that sent me bears witness of me."

Then they asked him, "Where is your Father? Yahshua answered, "You neither know me, or My Father. If you had known me, you should have known my Father also." These words Yahshua spoke in the treasury, as He taught in the Temple and no man laid hands on Him, for His hour had not yet come.

Then Yahshua said to them, "I go my way, and ye shall seek me, and shall die in your sins. Whither I go you cannot come." Then the Elders said, "Will he kill himself? Because He said, 'whither I go you cannot come.'" He said to them, "You are from beneath, I am from above. You are of the world I am not of the world. I said to you, 'That you shall die in your sins.' If you believe not that I am you shall die in your sins."

Then they said to Him, "Who are you?" Yahshua said to them, "Even that I said to you from the beginning. I have many things to say and to judge of you, but He that sent me is true and I speak to the world those things which I have heard of Him." They understood not that He spoke to them of the Father.

Then said Yahshua to them, When you have lifted up the Son of Man, then shall you know that I am, and I do nothing of myself, but as the Father has taught me, I speak these things. He that sent me is with me. The Father has not left me alone, for I always do those things that please Him. As He spoke these words many believed on Him

Then said Yahshua to those rulers who believed on Him, "If you continue in my word, you are my disciples indeed, and you shall know the truth and the truth shall make you free." They answered Him, "We are of Abraham's seed, and we have never been in bondage to any man. How is it you say, "You shall be made free?"

Yahshua answered them, "Verily I say to you, whoever commits sin is the servant of sin. The servant abides not in the house forever. The Son abides forever. If the Son shall make you free, you shall be free indeed.

I know that you are Abraham's seed, but you seek to kill me because my word has no place in you. I speak that which I have seen with my Father, and you do that which you have seen with your father."

They answered and said to Him, "Abraham is our father." Yahshua said to them, "If you were Abraham's children, you would do the works of Abraham. But now ye seek to kill me, a man that has told you the truth, which I have heard of God. This Abraham did not do. You do the deeds of your father."

Then said they to Him, "We are not born of fornication we have one Father, God." Yahshua said to them, "If God were your Father, you would love me, for I proceeded forth and came from God. Neither did I come of myself, but He sent me. Why do you not understand my speech? Because you cannot hear my word you are of your father, the devil, and the lusts of your father you will do.

He was a murderer from the beginning, and abode not in the truth, because there is no truth in him. When he spoke a lie, he speaks of his own. He is a liar and the father of it. Because I tell the truth, you believe me not."

"Which of you convinces me of sin? If I say the truth, why do you not believe me? He that is of God hears God's words. You do not hear because you are not of God. Then answered the rulers and said to Him, "Say we not well that you are a Samaritan, and have a devil?"

Yahshua answered, "I have not a devil, but I honor my Father, and you dishonor me. I do not seek mine own glory. There is one that seeks and judges. Verily, verily, I say to you, if a man keeps my saying, he shall never see death."

Then said the rulers to Him, "Now we know that you have a devil, Abraham is dead, and the prophets, and you say, 'If a man keep my saying he shall never taste of death.' Are you greater than our father Abraham, which is dead? And the prophets are dead. Who do you make yourself to be?"

Yahshua answered, "If I honor myself, my honor is nothing, it is my Father that honors me, of whom you say, that He is your God. Yet you have not known Him, but I know Him, and if I should say, I do not know Him, I shall be a liar like you. But I know Him, and keep His sayings. Your father Abraham rejoiced to see my day, and he saw it and was glad." Then the rulers said to Him, "You are not yet fifty years old, and have you seen Abraham?"

Yahshua said to them, "Verily, verily, I say to you, before Abraham was, I AM." Then they took up stones to cast at Him, but Yahshua hid Himself and went out of the Temple going through the midst of them, and so passed by.

As He passed by, He saw a man who was blind from birth. His disciples asked Him, saying, "Master, who did sin, this man, or his parents that he was born blind?"

Yahshua answered, "Neither has this man sinned, nor his parents, but that the works of Yahweh should be made manifest in him. I must work the works of Him that sent me while it is day. The night comes when no man can work. As long as I am in the world, I am the light of the world."

When He had thus spoken, He spat on the ground, and made clay of the spittle, and anointed the eyes of the blind man with clay, and said to him, "Go wash in the pool of Siloam," (Which is by interpretation, 'Sent').

He went his way and washed, and came seeing. The neighbors therefore, and they which before had seen him that was blind, said, "Is not this he that sat and begged?" Some said, "This is he." Others, "He is like him." He said, "I am he." They said to him, "How were your eyes opened?" He answered and said, "A man called Yahshua made clay and anointed mine eyes, and said to me, 'Go to the pool of Siloam and wash,' and I went and washed, and I received my sight." Then they said to him, "Where is He?" He said, "I don't know."

They brought him to the Pharisees that had been blind. It was the Sabbath when Yahshua made the clay, and opened his eyes. Then the Pharisees also asked him how he had received his sight. He said to them, "He put clay upon mine eyes and I washed, and now I can see."

Some of the Pharisees said, "This man is not of God, because He does not keep the Sabbath." Others said, "How can a man that is a sinner do such miracles?" There was a division among them. They said to the blind man again, "What do you say of Him, that He has opened your eyes? He said, "He is a Prophet."

But the Pharisees did not believe this concerning him that he had been blind, and received his sight, until they called the parents of him that had received his sight. And they asked them, saying, "Is this your son who you say was born blind? How then does he now see?"

His parents answered them and said, "We know that this is our son, and that he was born blind, but by what means he now sees, we know not, or who has opened his eyes, we know not. He is of age ask him, he can speak for himself."

His parents spoke in this manner because they feared the Pharisees, for the Pharisees had agreed already that 'if any man did confess that He was the Messiah, he should be put out of the synagogue. Therefore his parents said, "He is of age, ask him."

Then again they called the man that was blind, and said to him, "Give God the praise, we know that this man is a sinner." He answered and said, "Whether He is a sinner, I know not. One thing I do know is that, whereas I was blind, and now I can see." They said to him again, "What did He do to you? How did He open your eyes?"

He answered them, "I have told you already, and you did not hear. Why would you want to hear it again? Do you also want to be His disciples?" They answered him, "We know that God spoke to Moses. As for this man we do not know not from whence He comes."

The man answered and said to them, "Why herein is a marvelous thing that you do not know from whence He is, and He has opened mine eyes. Now we know that God does not hear sinners, but if any man is a worshipper of God, and does His will, God will hear him."

"Since the world began it has never been heard that any man opened the eyes of one that was born blind. If this man were not of God, He could do nothing." They answered and said to him. "You were altogether born in sins, and you think you can teach us?" And they cast him out of the Temple.

Yahshua heard that they had cast him out, and when He had found him, He said to him, "Do you believe on the Son of God?" He answered and said, "Who is He, Lord that I might believe on Him?" Yahshua said to him, "You have both seen Him, and it is He that talks with you." He said, "Lord, I believe." And he worshipped Him.

CHAPTER VII

Yahshua said, "For judgment I have come into this world, that they which do not see might see and that they which see might be made blind." When the Pharisees who were with Him heard these words, they said to Him, "Are we blind also?"

Yahshua said to them, "If you were blind, you would have no sin, but now you say, 'We see,' therefore your sin remains in you. Verily, verily, I say to you, He that does not enter by the door into the sheepfold, but climbs up some other way, the same is a thief and a robber."

"He that enters in by the door is the Shepherd of the sheep. To Him the porter opens, and the sheep hear His voice, and He calls His own sheep. He goes before them, and the sheep follow Him, for they know His voice. They will not follow a stranger, but will flee from him, for they do not know the voice of strangers."

Yahshua spoke this parable to them, but they did not understand the things which He spoke to them. Yahshua said to them again, "Verily, verily, I say to you, I am the door of the sheep. All that ever came before me are thieves and robbers, but the sheep do not hear them. I am the door, by me if any man enters in, he shall be saved, and shall go in and out, and find pasture. The thief comes not, but for to steal, and to kill, and to destroy."

"I am come that they might have life, and that they might have life more abundantly. I am the Good Shepherd. The Good Shepherd gives His life for the sheep. But he that is a hireling, and not the Shepherd, whose own sheep they are not, sees the wolf coming, and leaves the sheep, and flees, and the wolf catches them, and scatters the sheep. The hireling flees, because he is a hireling, and cares not for the sheep."

"I am the Good Shepherd, and know my sheep and am known of mine. As the Father knows me, even so know I the Father, and I lay down my life for the sheep. Other sheep I have, which are not of this fold. I must also bring them and they shall hear my voice, and there shall be one fold, and one Shepherd."

"I lay down my life that I might take it again. No man takes it from me, but I lay it down of myself, I have power to lay it down, and I have power to take it again. This commandment have I received of my Father."

There was a division again among the Pharisees concerning these things. Many of them said, "He has a devil, and is mad, why bother to hear Him?" Others said, "These are not the words of one that has a devil. Can a devil open the eyes of the blind?"

Now it came to pass, as they went, that Yahshua entered into a certain village, and a certain woman named Martha received Him into her house, she had a sister called Mary, who also sat at Yahshua's feet, and heard His word.

Martha was cumbered about with much serving, and came to Yahshua and said, "Lord, don't you care that my sister has left me to serve alone? Bid her therefore that she helps me." Yahshua answered and said unto her, "Martha, Martha, you are careful and troubled about many things. But one thing is needful, and Mary has chosen that good part, which shall not be taken away from her."

He was casting out a devil, and it was dumb. And it came to pass, when the devil was gone out, the dumb spoke, and the Pharisees wondered. But some of them said, "He casts out devils through Beelzebub the chief of the devils." Others, tempting, sought a sign of Him from heaven.

But Yahshua, knowing their thoughts, said to them, "Every Kingdom divided against it is brought to desolation. A house divided against a house falls. If Satan is divided against himself, how shall his kingdom stand? Because you say that I cast out devils through Beelzebub. If I by Beelzebub cast out devils, by whom do your sons cast them out?"

"Therefore shall they be your judges. But if I, with the finger of Yahweh cast out devils, no doubt the Kingdom of Yahweh has come upon you. When a strong man armed keeps his palace, his goods are in peace. But when a stronger than he shall come upon him, and overcome him, he takes from him all his armor wherein he trusted, and divides his spoils. He that is not with me is against me, and he that gathers not with me scatters."

When the unclean spirit is gone out of a man, he walks through dry places seeking rest, and finding none, he says, 'I will return to my house from whence I came.' And when he comes he finds it swept, and garnished. Then he goes and takes seven other spirits more wicked than himself, they enter in, and dwell there. The last condition of that man is worse than the first."

As He spoke these things, a certain woman of the company lifted up her voice, and said to Him, "Blessed is the womb that bare you, and the breasts which you have sucked." But He said, "Yea, rather, blessed are they that hear the Word of Yahweh, and keep it."

As He spoke, a certain Pharisee besought Him to dine with him and He went in, and sat down to meat. And when the Pharisee saw, he marveled that He had not first washed before dinner. The Lord said to him, "You Pharisees make clean the outside of the cup and the platter, but your inward part is full of ravening and wickedness. Fools, did not He that made that which is without, also make that which is within?"

"But rather give alms of such things as you have, and behold, all things are clean to you. Woe to you, Pharisees! You tithe mint and rue and all manner of herbs, and pass over judgment and the love of Yahweh. These you should have done, and not to leave the other undone."

"Woe to you, Pharisees! For you love the uppermost seats in the Synagogues, and greetings in the markets. Woe to you, Scribes and Pharisees, hypocrites! You are as graves which appear not, and the men that walk over you are not aware."

Then answered one of the lawyers, and said to Him, "Master, with this saying you reproach us also." Yahshua replied, "Woe to you lawyers also! You laden men with burdens grievous to be borne, and you yourselves touch not the burdens with one of your fingers."

"Woe to you! For you build the sepulchers of the prophets, and your fathers killed them, truly you bear witness that you allow the deeds of your fathers. For they indeed killed them and you built their sepulchers."

"Therefore the Wisdom of Yahweh also said, 'I will send them Prophets and Apostles and of them they shall slay and persecute.'" That the blood of all the prophets, which was shed from the foundation of the world, may be required of this generation, from the blood of Abel to the blood of Zechariah, which perished between the altar and the Temple."

"Verily I say to you, 'It shall be required of this generation.' Woe to you lawyers! You have taken away the key of knowledge. You did not enter in yourselves, and they that were entering in you hindered."

As He said these things to them, the Scribes and the Pharisees began to urge vehemently, and to provoke Him to speak of many things, laying wait for Him, and seeking to catch something out of His mouth, that they might accuse him.

It was at Jerusalem, during Chanukah, the Festival of Lights and Dedication, and it was winter. And Yahshua walked in the Temple in Solomon's Porch.

Then came the Chief Priests round about Him, and said to Him, "How long will you make us to doubt? If you are the Messiah, tell us plainly." Yahshua answered them, "I told you, and you did not believe me. The works that I do in my Father's Name, they bear witness of me, but you did not believe because you are not of my sheep, as I said to you, 'My sheep hear my voice, and I know them and they follow me.'"

"I give to them eternal life, and they shall never perish neither shall any pluck them out of my hand. My Father, who gave them to me, is greater than all, and none is able to pluck them out of my Father's hand. I and the Father are One.

Then the Chief Priests took up stones again to stone Him. Yahshua asked them, "Many good works I have shown you from my Father. For which of these works do you stone me?" The Chief Priests answered Him, saying, "For a good work we do not stone you, but for blasphemy, and because that you, being a man, make yourself to be God."

Yahshua answered them, "Is it not written in your law, 'I said you are gods?' He called them gods, to whom the Word of God came, and the Scripture cannot be broken. You say of Him, whom the Father has sanctified, and sent into the world, 'You blaspheme' because I said, I am the Son of God?"

"If I don't do the works of my Father believe me not, but if I do the works of my Father, though you do not believe me, believe the works, that you may know, and believe, that the Father is in me, and I am in Him."

Therefore they sought again to take Him, but He escaped out of their hand, and went away again beyond Jordan into the place where John at first baptized, and there He abode. Many resorted to Him and said, "John did no miracle, but everything that John spoke of this man is true." And many believed on Him there.

After six days Yahshua took Peter, James and John, and lead them up into a high mountain apart by themselves, and He was transfigured before them, His face did shine as the sun, and His raiment became shining, exceedingly white as snow, so as no fuller on earth can white them.

There appeared to them Elijah with Moses, and they were talking with Yahshua and spoke of His decease which He would accomplish at Jerusalem. Peter and they that were with him were heavy with sleep. When they awaken they saw His glory, and the two men that stood with Him.

It came to pass, as they departed from Him, that Peter said to Yahshua, "Master, it is good for us to be here. Let us make three tabernacles, one for you, one for Moses and one for Elijah." For he did not know what to say because they were sore afraid. While he yet spoke, behold, a bright cloud overshadowed them, and behold a voice came out of the cloud saying, "This is my Beloved Son, in whom I am well pleased, hear Him."

When the disciples heard, they fell on their faces and were very much afraid. Suddenly, when they had looked round about, they saw no one anymore, save for Yahshua only with themselves. Yahshua came and touched them, and said, "Arise, and be not afraid."

As they came down from the mountain, Yahshua charged them, saying, "Tell the vision to no man, until the Son of Man be risen again from the dead," And they kept that saying within themselves questioning one with another what the rising from the dead should mean.

They asked Him, saying, "Why then say the Scribes that Elijah must come first? " Yahshua answered and said to them, "Elijah truly shall first come, and restore all things. I say to you that Elijah has come already, and they knew him not, but have done with him whatsoever they listed."

"Likewise, it is written of the Son of Man that He must suffer many things and be set at naught. Then the disciples understood that He spoke to them of John the Baptist.

When He came to His disciples, He saw a great multitude about them, and the Scribes questioning with them. All the people, when they beheld Him, were greatly amazed, and running to Him saluted Him. He asked the Scribes, "What do you question with them about?"

There came to Him one of the multitude who answered and said, "Master have mercy on my son, for he is lunatic, and sore vexed by a dumb spirit, and wherever he takes him, he tears him, and he foams at the mouth, and gnashes with his teeth, and pines away. I spoke to your disciples that they should cast out the dumb spirit and they could not cure him."

Yahshua answered and said, "O faithless and perverse generation. How long shall I be with you? Bring him to me." And they brought the boy to Him, and when the dumb spirit saw Yahshua, straightway it tare the boy and he fell to the ground, and wallowed, foaming at the mouth.

Yahshua asked his father, "How long has it been since this came upon him?" He said, "Since he was a child. And often times it has cast him into the fire, and into the waters, to destroy him, but if you can do anything have compassion on us and help us."

Yahshua said to him, "If you can believe, all things are possible to him that believes." Straightway the father of the child cried out, and said with tears, "Lord, I believe, help mine unbelief." When Yahshua saw that the people came running together, He rebuked the foul spirit, saying to him, "Dumb and deaf spirit, I charge you, come out of him, and enter no more into him."

The foul spirit cried, and rent him sore, and came out of him, and he lay as one dead insomuch that many said, "He is dead." But Yahshua took him by the hand, lifted him up, and he arose.

When Yahshua came into the house, His disciples asked Him privately, "Why couldn't we cast him out?" He said to them, "This kind can come forth by nothing, but by prayer and fasting"

They departed from there, and passed through Galilee, and He would not that any man should know. He taught His disciples, and said to them, "The Son of Man shall be betrayed and delivered into the hands of men, and they shall kill

Him, and after He is killed, He shall rise the third day." But they did not understand this saying, and it was hid from them, they did not perceive its meaning, and they were exceedingly sorry and they feared to ask Him what it meant.

Yahshua came to Capernaum, and being in the house He asked them, "What was it that you disputed among yourselves by the way?" But they held their peace, for by the way they had disputed amongst themselves, as to who should be the greatest. He sat down, and called the twelve, and said to them, "If any man desires to be first, he must be last of all, and servant to all."

Yahshua called a little child to Him, and set him in the midst of them, and when He had taken him in His arms, He said to them, "Whoever shall receive one of such children in my Name, receives me, and whoever shall receive me, receives not me, but Him that sent me. Verily I say to you, except you be converted, and become as little children, you shall not enter into the Kingdom of Heaven."

"Whoever shall humble himself as this little child, the same is greatest in the Kingdom of Heaven. But whoever shall offend one of these little ones who believe in me, it would be better for him that a millstone was hung about his neck, and that he was cast into the depth of the sea."

"Woe to the world because of offenses! It must be that offenses come, but woe to that man by whom the offense comes! If your hand or your foot offend you, cut them off and cast them from you, it is better for you to enter into life hall or maimed, rather than having two hands or two feet and to be cast into everlasting fire."

"If your eye offend you pluck it out, and cast it from you, it is better for you to enter into life with one eye, rather than having two eyes to be cast into hell, into the fire that never shall be quenched, where their worm never dies and the fire is never quenched."

"Everyone shall be salted with fire, and every sacrifice shall be salted with salt. Salt is good, but if the salt has lost its saltiness, how will you season it? Have salt in yourselves, and have peace one with another."

Then came Peter to Him, and said, 'Lord, how often shall my brother sin against me, and I forgive him? Till seven times?' Yahshua said to him, "I say not to you until seven times, but until seventy times seven."

"Therefore is the Kingdom of Heaven likened to a certain king who would take account of his servants. And when he had begun to reckon, one was brought unto him which owed him ten thousand talents. But forasmuch as he had nothing to pay his lord commanded him to be sold, and his wife, and children, and all that he had, and payment to be made."

"The servant fell down, and worshipped him, saying, 'Lord, have patience with me, and I will pay you all.' The lord of that servant was moved with compassion, and loosed him, and forgave him the debt."

"But the same servant went out, and found one of his fellow servants, which owed him a hundred pence, and he laid hands on him, and took him by the throat, saying, 'Pay me that which you owe me.' His fellow servant fell down at his feet, and besought him saying, 'Have patience with me and I will pay you all.'"

"And he would not, but went and cast him into prison, until he should pay the debt. When his fellow servants saw what was done, they were very sorry, and came and told to their lord all that was done."

"His lord, after he had called him, said to him, 'O wicked servant, I forgave you all that debt, because you desired it of me. Should not you also have had compassion on your fellow servant, even as I had pity on you?'"

"His lord was angry with him and delivered him to the tormentors, until he should pay all that was due to him. So likewise shall my heavenly Father do to you, if from your hearts you do not forgive everyone his brother their trespasses."

"Take heed to yourselves, if your brother trespass against you, rebuke him, and if he repent, forgive him. If he trespasses against you seven times in a day, and seven times in a day turn again, crying, 'I repent,' you must forgive him."

Moreover, if your brother shall trespass against you, go and tell him his fault between you and him alone, if he shall hear you, you have gained your brother. But if he will not hear, take with you one or two more, that in the mouth of two or three witnesses every word may be established."

"If he refuses to hear them, tell it to the assembly, and if he neglects to hear the assembly, let him be to you as a heathen man and a publican."

"Verily, I say to you, whatever you shall bind on earth shall be bound in heaven, and whatever you shall loose on earth shall be loosed in heaven. Again, I say to you, that if two of you shall agree on earth as touching anything that they shall ask, it shall be done for them of my Father which is in heaven."

"Where two or three are gathered together in my Name, there am I in the midst of them. The apostles said to the Lord, "Increase our faith." Yahshua said, "If you had faith as a grain of mustard seed, you might say to this sycamore tree, 'Be plucked up by the root, and be planted in the sea,' and it should obey you."

And when they came to Capernaum, they that received tribute came to Peter, and said, "Doesn't your Master pay tribute?" He said, "Yes." When he came into the house Yahshua prevented him, saying, "What do you think, Simon? Of whom do the kings of the earth take custom or tribute, of their own children or of strangers?" Peter said to Him, "Of strangers."

"Yahshua said to him, "Then are the children free. Notwithstanding, lest we should offend them, go to the sea, and cast a hook, and take up the fish that first comes up, and when you have opened his mouth, you will find a piece of money, take that, and give it to them for you and me."

The Pharisees, who were covetous, when they had heard all these things, ridiculed Him. He said to them, "You are they which justify yourselves before men, but Yahweh knows your hearts, for that which is highly esteemed among men is an abomination in the sight of Yahweh."

"The law and the prophets were until John, since that time the Kingdom of God is preached and every man presses into it. It is easier for heaven and earth to pass, than one tittle of the law to fail."

And John answered Him, saying, "Master, we saw one casting out devils in your Name, and he did not follow us, and we forbid him, because he did not follow with us." Yahshua said to him, "Forbid him not, for there is no man who shall do a miracle in my Name that can lightly speak evil of me. He that is not against us is on our part for us, for whoever shall give you a cup of water to drink in my Name, because you belong to the Messiah, verily I say to you, he shall not lose his reward."

The people brought their young children to Him, that He should touch them, and His disciples rebuked them. When Yahshua saw what they were doing, He was very much displeased with them, and said to his disciples, "Suffer the little children to come to me, and forbid them not, for of such is the Kingdom of God. Verily I say to you, whoever shall not receive the Kingdom of Yahweh as a little child, he shall not enter therein." He took the children up in His arms, lay hands on them, and blessed them.

When He was gone forth into the way, there came one running, and kneeling to Him asked, "Good Master, what shall I do that I may inherit eternal life?" Yahshua said to him, "Why do you call me good? There is none that is good but one, Yahweh. You know the commandments, do not commit adultery, do not kill, do not steal, do not bear false witness, defraud not, and honor your father and mother."

"And he answered and said to Yahshua, "Master, all these have I observed from my youth." Then Yahshua, beholding him loved him, and said to him, "One thing you lack, go your way, sell whatever you have, give to the poor, and you will have treasure in heaven, and come follow me."

When he heard this, he was very sorrowful, for he was very rich and had great possessions. Yahshua looked round about, and said to His disciples, "How with difficulty shall they who have riches enter into the Kingdom of Yahweh!"

His disciples were astonished at His words. Yahshua answered again, and said to them, "Children, how with difficulty it is for them that trust in riches to enter into the Kingdom of Yahweh. It is easier for a camel to go through the eye of a needle, than for a rich man to enter into the Kingdom of Yahweh."

They were astonished out of measure, saying among themselves, "Who then can be saved?" Yahshua, looking upon them said, "With men it is impossible, but with God all things are possible."

Then Peter began to say to Him. "Lo, we have left all, and have followed you." Yahshua answered and said, "Verily I say to you, there is no man that has left house, or brethren, or sisters, or father, or mother, or wife, or children, or lands, for my sake, and the gospel's, but he shall receive a hundredfold now in this time, houses, and brethren, and sisters, and mother, and children, and lands, with persecutions, and in the World to Come, eternal life. Many who are first shall be last and the last first."

They were on the way to Jerusalem, and Yahshua went before them, and they were amazed, and as they followed, they were afraid. He once again took the twelve apart, and began to tell them what things would happen to Him, "Behold, we go up to Jerusalem, and the Son of Man shall be delivered to the Chief Priests and the Scribes, and they shall condemn Him to death, and they shall deliver Him to the Gentiles, they will mock Him, and spit upon Him, and shall kill Him, and on the third day He shall rise again."

One of the company said to Him, "Master, speak to my brother, that he divide the inheritance with me." He said to him, "Man, who made me a judge or a divider over you?" He said to them, "Take heed, and beware of covetousness, for a man's life consists not in the abundance of the things which he possesses."

He spoke a parable to them, saying, "The ground of a certain rich man brought forth plentifully, and he thought within himself saying, 'What will I do, because I have no room where to bestow my fruits?' And he said, 'This is what I will do. I will pull down my barns and build greater, and there will I bestow all my fruits and my goods. I will say to my soul, soul, you have much goods laid up for many years, take your ease, eat, drink, be merry.'"

"But Yahweh said to him, 'Fool, this night your soul shall be required of you. Then whose shall those things be, which you have provided?' So is he that lays up treasure for himself, and is not rich towards Yahweh.'"

There came to Him the mother of Zebedee's children with her sons James and John, worshipping and desiring a certain thing of Him. He said to her, 'What wilt you that I shall do for you?" She said to Him, "Grant me that these my two sons may sit, the one on your right hand and the other on your left in your Kingdom."

But Yahshua said to them, "You do not know what you have asked for. Can you drink of the cup that I drink of? And be baptized with the baptism that I am baptized with?" They said to Him, "We can." Yahshua said to them, "You shall indeed drink of the cup that I drink of, and with the baptism that I am baptized with shall you be baptized, but to sit on my right hand and on my left hand is not mine to give, but is reserved for those for whom it has been prepared."

When the ten heard this discussion, they began to be much displeased with James and John. But Yahshua called them together and said to them, "You know that they which are accounted to rule over the Gentiles exercise lordship over them, and their great ones exercise authority upon them. But so it shall not be among you. Whoever wants to be great among you shall be your minister, and whoever wants to be the chief shall be servant to all. Even the Son of Man came not to be ministered to, but to minister, and to give His life a ransom for many."

And it came to pass as He came nigh to Jericho, a certain blind man sat by the wayside begging, blind Bartimeus, the son of Timeus. When he heard that it was Yahshua of Nazareth, he began to cry out, and say, "Yahshua, son of David, have mercy on me."

Many charged him that he should hold his peace, but he cried the more a great deal, "Son of David, have mercy on me." Yahshua stood still, and commanded that the blind man be brought to Him. They called to the blind man saying to him, "Be of good comfort, rise He calls for you."

He, casting away his garment rose and came to Yahshua. Yahshua asked him saying, "What do you want me to do for you?" The blind man said to Him, "Lord, that I might receive my sight." Yahshua said to him," Go your way, your faith has made you whole." Immediately he received his sight, and followed Yahshua in the way, glorifying Yahweh. All the people, when they saw what had been done, gave praise to Yahweh.

Yahshua entered and passed through Jericho. And behold, a man named Zaccheus, who was the chief among publicans, and very rich, sought to see who Yahshua was, could not for the press, because he was little of stature. He ran before the crowd and climbed up into a sycamore tree to see Yahshua, because He was to pass that way.

When Yahshua came to the place, where Zaccheus was, He looked up, and saw him, and said to him, "Zaccheus, make haste, and come down, for today I must abide at your house. Zaccheus made haste and came down from the tree and received Him joyfully. When they saw they all murmured, saying that He was gone to be guest with a man that is a sinner."

Zaccheus stood and said to Yahshua, "Behold Lord, the half of my goods I give to the poor, and if I have taken anything from any man by false accusation, I will it restore fourfold." Yahshua said to him, "This day salvation has come to this house forasmuch as he also is a son of Abraham. For the Son of Man is come to seek and to save that which was lost."

Now a certain man was sick, Lazarus, of Bethany, the town of Mary and her sister Martha. (This was Mary who had anointed the Lord with ointment, and wiped his feet with her hair, whose brother Lazarus was sick). Therefore his sisters sent to Him, saying, "Lord, behold, he whom you love is sick."

When Yahshua heard this He said, "This sickness is not unto death, but that the glory of Yahweh, and the Son of Yahweh might be glorified thereby." Now Yahweh loved Martha, and her sister and Lazarus.

When He heard therefore that Lazarus was sick, He abode two days still in the same place where He was. After that He said to the disciples, "Let us go into Judea again." The disciples said to Him, "Master, the Chief Priests have recently sought to stone you, and do you now go there again?"

Yahshua answered, "Are there not twelve hours in the day? If any man walks in the day, he does not stumble, because he sees the light of this world. But if a man walks in the night, he stumbles, because there is no light in him."

After He had spoken these things to them He said, "Our friend Lazarus sleeps, but I go that I may awaken him out of his sleep." His disciples then said to Him, "Lord, if he sleeps, he shall do well." Howbeit Yahshua spoke of his death, but they thought that He had spoken of taking of rest in sleep. Yahshua then spoke to them plainly." Lazarus is dead. I am glad for your sakes that I was not there to the intent you might believe. Nevertheless let us go to him."

Then Thomas, who is called Didymus, said to his fellow disciples, "Let us also go, so that we may die with him." When Yahshua came, He found that Lazarus had already lain in the cave four days.

Now Bethany was close to Jerusalem, about fifteen furlongs off, and many people came to Martha and Mary, to comfort them concerning their brother. As soon as Martha heard that Yahshua had come went to meet Him, but Mary remained sitting in the house.

Then Martha spoke to Yahshua, "Lord, if you had been here, my brother would not have died. But I know, that even now, whatever you ask of Yahweh, He will give it to you." Yahshua said to her, "Your brother will rise again."

Martha said to Him, "I know that he will rise again in the resurrection at the last day." Yahshua said to her, "I am the resurrection, and the life, he that believes in me, though he were dead, yet shall he live, and whoever lives and believes in me shall never die. Do you believe this?" She said to Him, "Yes Lord, I believe that you are the Messiah, the Son of Yahweh who shall come into the world."

When she had so said, she went her way, and called Mary her sister secretly, saying, "The Master has come, and calls for you." As soon as she heard this, Mary arose quickly, and went to Him.

Yahshua had not yet come into the town but was still in that place where Martha had met Him. The people who were with her in the house, and had comforted her, when they saw Mary, that she rose up hastily and went out, followed her, saying, "She goes to the grave to weep there."

When Mary came where Yahshua was, and saw Him, she fell down at His feet, saying to Him, "Lord, if you had been here, my brother would not have died. When Yahshua saw her weeping, and the people also weeping which came with her, He groaned in the spirit, and was troubled, and said, "Where have you laid him? They said to Him, "Lord, come and see." Yahshua wept. The people said, "Behold how much He loved him." However, some of them said, "Could not this man, which opened the eyes of the blind, have caused that even this man should not have died?

Yahshua again groaning in Himself came to the grave. It was a cave, and a stone lay upon it. Yahshua said, "Take away the stone." Martha, the sister of him that was dead, said to Him, "Lord, by this time he stinks, for he has been in the cave for four days." Yahshua said to her, "Did I not say to you, that, if you would believe, you would see the glory of Yahweh?" Then they took away the stone where the dead body was laid.

Yahshua lifted up His eyes and said, "Father, I thank You that You have heard me. And I know that You hear me always, but because of the people who stand by I have spoken so that they may believe that You have sent me,"

After He had spoken, He cried with a loud voice, "Lazarus, come forth." And he that was dead came forth, bound hand and foot with grave clothes, and his face was bound about with a napkin. Yahshua said to them, "Loose him, and let him go,"

Many of the people who came with Mary, and had seen the things which Yahshua had done believed on Him. But some of them went to the Pharisees, and told them what Yahshua had done, The Chief Priests and the Pharisees gathered together a council, and said, "What shall we do?

This man does many miracles. If we let him alone all the people will believe on him and the Romans will come and take away both our place and our nation."

One of them, Caiaphas, being the High Priest that same year, said to them, "You know nothing at all, nor consider that it is expedient for us, that one man should die for the people, and that the whole nation should not perish." This he spoke although not of himself, but being High Priest that year, he prophesied that Yahshua should die for the nation, and not for that nation only, but that He would also gather together in one the children of Yahweh that were scattered abroad. From that day forth they took counsel together to put Him to death.

CHAPTER VIII

Yahshua did not walk openly among the Judeans, but went to a country near to the wilderness into a city called Ephraim, and there continued with His disciples. The Passover was close at hand, and many went out of the country up to Jerusalem before the Passover, to purify themselves.

They looked for Yahshua and spoke among themselves as they stood in the Temple, "Do you think that He will not come to the Feast?" Now both the Chief Priests and the Pharisees had given commandment that, if any man knew where He was, he should reveal it so that they might take Him prisoner.

Six days before the Passover Yahshua came to Bethany, where Lazarus was who had been dead, whom Yahshua raised from the dead. There they made Him a supper, and Martha served, but Lazarus was one of them that sat at the table with Him, being in the house of Simon the Leper.

As He sat at meat, Mary came to Him with an alabaster box of ointment of spikenard very precious, she broke the box and poured it on His head, and anointed the feet of Yahshua and wiped His feet with her hair, and the house was filled with the odor of the ointment.

One of his disciples, Judas Iscariot, Simon's son, who would betray Him, asked, "Why wasn't this ointment sold for three hundred pence, and given to the poor?" This he said, not that he cared for the poor, but because he was a thief, and had the bag, and bear what was put therein.

Yahshua said, "Let her alone, against the day of my burying has she kept this. The poor you will always have with you, but me you will not always have. Verily I say to you, 'Wherever this gospel shall be preached throughout the whole world, also that she hath done shall be spoken of for a memorial of her."

Much people therefore knowing that He was there, came not for Yahshua's sake only, but that they might see Lazarus whom He had raised from the dead. But the Chief Priests consulted that they might also put Lazarus to death, because by reason of him many of the people went away, and believed on Yahshua.

The next day they drew nigh to Jerusalem, and came to Bethpage to the Mount of Olives. Yahshua sent two disciples, saying to them, "Go into the village over against you, and straightway you shall find an ass tied, and a colt with her, whereon never man sat, loose him and bring to me. If any man says to you, 'Why do you do this?' Say that the Lord has need of him, and straightway he will send him here."

They went their way, and found the colt tied by the door in a place where two ways met, and they loosed him. This was done, that it might be fulfilled which was spoken by the prophet, saying, "Tell the daughter of Zion, 'Behold your King comes to you, meek, and sitting upon an ass, and a colt the foal of an ass.'"

As they were losing the colt, the owners thereof said to them, "Why do you loose the colt?" They answered, "The Lord has need of him." They brought him to Yahshua, and they cast their garments upon the colt, and Yahshua sat upon him. A great multitude, when they heard that Yahshua was coming to Jerusalem took branches of palm trees, and went forth to meet Him, spreading their garments in the way, and cried, saying, "Hosanna, Blessed is He that comes in the Name of the Lord. Blessed be the kingdom of David, that comes in the Name of the Lord. Hosanna in the highest."

When He came nigh, even now at the descent of the Mount of Olives, the whole multitude of the disciples began to rejoice and praise Yahweh with a loud voice for all the mighty works they had seen, saying, "Blessed be the King that comes in the Name of the Lord, peace in Heaven and glory in the highest."

Some of the Pharisees from among the multitudes said to Him, "Master, rebuke your disciples." He answered and said to them, "I tell you that, if these should hold their peace, the stones would immediately cry out."

These things His disciples did not understand at first, but when Yahshua was glorified they remembered that these things were written about Him, and they had done these things to Him. The people that had been with Him when He called Lazarus out of the grave and raised him from the dead bear record. For this cause the people also met Him, for they heard that He had done this miracle.

The Pharisees therefore said among them, "Do you perceive how you do not prevail? Behold, the world is gone with Him." When He came into Jerusalem, the entire city was moved, saying, "Who is this?" The multitude said, "This is Yahshua, the prophet of Nazareth of Galilee."

When He came near, He beheld the city and wept over it, saying, "If you had known, even you, at least in this your day, the things to your peace! But now they are hid from your eyes. The days shall come upon you, that your enemies will cast a trench about you, and compass you round, and keep you in on every side, and shall lay you even with the ground, and your children within you, and they shall not leave in you one stone upon another because you did not know the time of your visitation."

Yahshua entered into Jerusalem and into the Temple and found in the Temple those that sold oxen and sheep, and doves, and the changers of money sitting, and when He had made a scourge of small cords, He drove them all out of the Temple, the sheep, and the oxen, and poured out the changers' money and overthrew the tables, and said to them that sold doves, "Take these things out of here and make not my Father's house a house of merchandise. It is written, 'My house shall be called of all nations the House of Prayer,' but you have made it a den of thieves"

The blind and the lame came to Him in the Temple, and He healed them. When the Chief Priests and the Scribes saw the wonderful things He did, and heard the children crying in the Temple, saying, "Hosanna to the Son of David," they were greatly displeased, and said to Him, "Do you hear what they say?"

Yahshua said to them, "Yes, and have you never read, 'out of the mouths of babes and infants you have perfected praise?"' The Scribes and Chief

Priests heard what He said, and sought how they might destroy him, because they feared Him, and because all the people were astonished at His doctrine.

When evening came He left them, and went out of the city into Bethany, and He lodged there. In the morning, as He came from Bethany and returned to the city, He hungered. When he saw a fig tree along the way He came to it and found nothing thereon, but leaves only. He said to it, "Let no fruit grow on you from now on forever." And presently the fig tree withered away.

There were certain Greek Jews among them that came up to worship during the Feast of Passover. The same came to Philip, who was of Bethsaida of Galilee, and desired of him saying, "Sir, we would see Yahshua." Philip came and told Andrew and Andrew and Philip told Yahshua. Yahshua answered them, saying, "The hour has come that the Son of Man shall be glorified. Verily, verily, I say to you except a grain of wheat fall into the ground and die, it abides alone, but if it dies, it brings forth much fruit."

"He that loves his life shall lose it, and he that hates his life in this world shall keep it unto life eternal. If any man serve me, let him follow me, and where I am, there shall also my servant be, if any man serve me, him will the Father honor."

Now is my soul troubled, and what shall I say? Father, save me from this hour, but for this cause come I to this hour. Father glorifies Your Name.

There came a voice from heaven, "I have both glorified it, and I will glorify it again." And the people that stood by heard, said that it thundered, others said, "An angel spoke to Him." Yahshua said, "This voice came not because of me, but for your sakes. Now is the judgment of this world, now shall the prince of this world be cast out. And I, if I be lifted up from the earth will draw all to me." This He said, signifying what death He should die.

The people answered Him, "We have heard out of the law that the Messiah abides forever, and how do you say, 'The Son of Man must be lifted up?' Who is this Son of Man?"

Yahshua said to them, "Yet a little while is the Light with you. Walk while you have the Light, lest darkness come upon you, for he that walks in darkness does not know where he goes. While you have the Light, believe in the Light, that you may be the children of Light." These things spoke Yahshua and departed, and did not hide from them.

He taught daily in the Temple. But the Chief Priests and the Scribes and the chief of the people sought to destroy Him, and could not find what they might do, for all the people were very attentive to hear Him. And it came to pass, on one of those days as He taught the people in the Temple, and preached the gospel, the Chief Priests and the Scribes came upon Him with the elders, and spoke to Him, saying, "Tell us, by what authority do you do these things? Or who is He that gave you this authority?"

He answered and said to them. "I will also ask you one thing, and answer me: The baptism of John was it from heaven, or of men?" They reasoned with themselves, saying, "If we say, 'From Heaven,' He will say, 'Why then did you not believe him?' If we say, 'Of men,' all the people will stone us, for they are persuaded that John was a prophet. They answered that they could not tell from where it came. Yahshua said to them, "Neither will I tell you by what authority I do these things."

He spoke this parable to them saying, "What man of you, having an hundred sheep, if he lose one of them, does not leave the ninety and nine in the wilderness, and go after that which is lost until he find it? And when he has found it he will lay it on his shoulders, rejoicing. And when He comes home, he calls together his friends and neighbors, saying to them, 'Rejoice with me, for I have found my sheep which was lost.' I say to you, that likewise joy shall be in heaven over one sinner that repents, more than over ninety and nine just persons, who have no need for repentance."

"Either what woman has ten pieces of silver, if she loses one piece, does, not light a candle, and sweep the house, and seek diligently until she finds it. And when she has found it, she calls her friends and neighbors together, saying, 'Rejoice with me, for I have found the piece which I lost,' Likewise, I say to you, there is joy in the presence of the angels of Yahweh over one sinner that repents?"

Yahshua said, "A certain man had two sons, and the younger of them said to his father, 'Father, give me the portion of goods that belongs to me', and the father separated to them his living. Not many days after wards the younger son gathered all that was his together, and took his journey into a far country, and there wasted all his substance with riotous living."

"When the younger son had spent all his substance, there arose a mighty famine in that land and he began to be in want. He went and joined himself to a citizen of that country, who sent him into the fields to feed his swine. The younger son would fain have filled his belly with the husks that the swine did eat, and no man gave to him. When he came to himself, he said, ''How many hired servants of my father have bread enough and to spare, and I perish with hunger! I will arise and go to my father, and will say to him, 'Father, I have sinned against heaven, and before you, and am no more worthy to be called your son, make me as one of your hired servants.'

"He arose, and came to his father. But when he was yet a great way off, his father saw him, and had compassion, and ran, and fell on his neck, and kissed him. And the son said to him, 'Father, I have sinned against heaven and in your sight, and am no more worthy to be called your son.'"

"But the father said to his servants, 'Bring forth the best robe, and put it on him, and put a ring on his hand, and shoes on his feet. And bring here the fatted calf, and let us eat, and be merry. For this my son was dead, and is alive again. He was lost, and is found,' and they began to be merry."

"Now his elder son was in the field, and as he came and drew nigh to the house, he heard music and dancing. He called one of the servants and asked what these things meant. The servant said to him, 'Your brother has come, and your father has killed the fatted calf, because he has received him safe and sound.'"

And he was angry, and would not go in therefore his father came out and entreated him. Answering he said to his father, 'Lo, these many years I have served you, neither have I transgressed at any time your commandment, and yet you never gave me a kid, that I might make merry with my friends. But as soon as this your son has come, who has devoured your living with harlots, you have killed for him the fatted calf.'"

The father said to him, 'Son, you are ever with me, and all that I have is yours. It was only correct that we should make merry, and be glad, for this your brother was dead, and is alive again, and was lost, and now is found.'"

Yahshua said to His disciples, "There was a certain rich man, who had a steward, and the same was accused to him that this servant had wasted his goods. He called the servant to him, and said, 'How is it that I hear this of you? Give an account of your stewardship, for you are no longer my steward,'"

"The steward said within himself, 'What shall I do? For my lord takes away from me the stewardship, I cannot dig, to beg I am ashamed. I am resolved what to do, that, when I am put out of the stewardship they may receive me into their houses.' So he called every one of his lord's debtors and said to the first, 'how much do you owe my lord?' And he said, 'An hundred measures of oil.' He said to him, 'Take your bill and sit down quickly, and write fifty.'"

"He then said to another, 'How much do you owe?' And he said, 'An hundred measures of wheat.' The unjust servant said to him, 'Take your bill, and write fourscore.' And the lord commended the unjust servant because he had done wisely. For the children of this world, are in their generation wiser than the children of light."

"I say to you, 'Make for yourselves friends of the mammon of unrighteousness, that, when you fail, they may receive you into everlasting habitations. He that is faithful in that which is least is faithful also in much. He that is unjust in the least is unjust also in much. If you have been unfaithful in unrighteous mammon, who will commit to your trust true righteousness? If you have not been faithful in that which is another man's, who will give you that which is your own?"

"No servant can serve two masters. Either he will hate the one, and love the other, or else he will hold to the one, and despise the other. You cannot serve Yahweh and mammon." The Pharisees also, who were covetous, heard all these things, and they derided Him.

He said to them, "You are they which justify yourselves before men, but Yahweh knows your hearts, for that which is highly esteemed among men is an abomination in the sight of Yahweh. The law and the prophets until John, since that time the Kingdom of Yahweh presses into it."

"It is easier for heaven and earth to pass, than one tittle of the law to fail. Whoever puts away his wife and marries commits adultery. And whoever marries her that is put away from her husband commits adultery."

"There was a certain rich man, who was clothed in purple and fine linen, and fared sumptuously every day. And there was a certain beggar named Lazarus, who lay at his gate, full of sores, and desired to be fed with the crumbs which fell from the rich man's table. Moreover the dogs came and licked his sores."

"It came to pass, that the beggar died, and was carried by angels into Abraham's bosom. The rich man also died, and was buried. In hell he lifted up his eyes, being in torments, and he could see Abraham afar off and Lazarus in his bosom. He cried out and said, 'Father Abraham, have mercy on me, and send Lazarus, that he may dip the tip of his finger in water, and cool my tongue, for I am tormented in this flame.'"

"But Abraham said, 'Son, remember that you in your lifetime you received good things, and likewise Lazarus evil things. But now he is comforted, and you are tormented. And besides all this there is a great gulf fixed between us and you so that they which would pass from here to you cannot, neither can they pass to us that would come from there.'"

"Then the rich man said, 'I therefore pray father that you would send him to my father's house. For I have five brethren. That he may testify to them, lest they also come into this place of torment.' Abraham said to him, 'They have Moses and the prophets, let them hear them.' The rich man said, 'Nay, father Abraham, but if one went to them from the dead, they will repent.'"

"Abraham said to the rich man, 'If they hear not Moses and the prophets, neither will they be persuaded, though one rose from the dead.'"

"But what do you think? A man had two sons, and he came to the first and said, 'Son, go work today in my vineyard.' And answered and said, 'I will not,' but afterward he repented, and went. And the father came to the second son, and said likewise, and he answered and said, 'I go, sir,' and went not. Which of the two did the will of the father?" They said to Him, "The first."

Yahshua said to them, "Verily I say to you, that the publicans and the harlots go into the Kingdom of Yahweh before you. John came to you in the way of righteousness, and you did not believe him, but the publicans and the harlots believed him, and you, when you had seen, repented not afterward, that you might believe him."

"Hear another parable. There was a certain householder, who planted a vineyard, and hedged it round about, and dug a winepress in it, and built a tower, and let it out to husbandmen, and went into a large country."

"When the time of the fruit drew near, he sent his servants to the husbandmen, that they might receive the fruits of it. The husbandmen took his servants and beat one, and killed another, and stoned another. Again, he sent other servants more than the first, and they did to them likewise."

"Last of all he sent his son, saying, 'They will reverence my son.' But when the husbandmen saw the son, they said among themselves, 'This is the heir, come, let us kill him, and let us seize on his inheritance.' They caught him, and cast him out of the vineyard, and slew him."

"When the lord therefore of the vineyard comes, what will he do to those husbandmen? They said to Him, "He will miserably destroy those wicked men, and will let out the vineyard to other husbandmen, who shall render him the fruits in their seasons."

Yahshua said to them, "Did you never read in the Scriptures, the stone which the builders rejected, the same has become the head of the corner, this is Yahweh's doing, and it is marvelous in our eyes? Therefore I say to you, the Kingdom of Yahweh shall be taken from you, and given to a nation bringing forth the fruits thereof. Whoever shall fall on this stone shall be broken, but on whoever it shall fall, it will grind him to powder."

Yahshua spoke to them again in parables, and said, "The Kingdom of Heaven is like a certain king, who made a marriage for his son. He sent forth his servants to call them that were bidden to the wedding, and they would not come. Again, he sent forth other servants, saying, 'Tell them which are bidden, Behold, I have prepared my dinner. My oxen and fatlings have been killed, and all things are made ready, come to the marriage.'"

"But they made light of it and went their ways, one to his farm, another to his merchandise, and the remnant took his servants, and entreated them spitefully, and slew them. When the king heard what had happened he was extremely angry, and he sent forth his armies, destroyed those murderers, and burned up their city."

"Then he said to his servants, 'The wedding is ready, but they which were bidden were not worthy. Go out quickly into the streets, and lanes of the city, and bring in the poor, the maimed, the halt, and the blind.' The servant said, 'Lord, it is done as you have commanded, and yet there is room.' The lord said to the servant, 'Go out into the highways and hedges, and compel to come in, that my house may be filled. For I say to you, that none of those men which were bidden shall taste of my supper.'"

"When the king came in to see the guests, he saw there a man who did not have on a wedding garment. He said to him, 'Friend, how did you come in here not having a wedding garment?' The guest was speechless. Then said the king to the servants, 'Bind him hand and foot, take him away, and cast him into outer darkness.' There shall be weeping and gnashing of teeth. Many are called but few are chosen."

The Chief Priests and the Scribes the same hour sought to lay hands on Him, but they feared the people, for they perceived that He had spoken against them. They watched, and sent forth spies, who would feign themselves just men so that they might take hold of His words, that so they might deliver Him into the power and the authority of the governor.

And they asked Him, saying, 'Master, we know that you say and teach rightly, neither do you accept the person, but teaches the way of Yahweh truly. Is it lawful for us to give tribute to Caesar, or not?' Yahshua perceived their craftiness, and said to them, "Why do you tempt me? Show me a penny, whose image and superscription is on it?" They answered and said, 'Caesar's'. He said to them, "Render therefore to Caesar the things which are Caesar's, and to Yahweh the things which are Yahweh's."

And they could not take hold of His words before the people, and they marveled at His answer, and held their peace. The same day the Sadducees came to Him who say that there is no resurrection, and asked Him, saying, "Master, Moses wrote to us, that if a man's brother die, and leave wife and no children, that his brother should take his wife, and raise up seed' to his brother."

"Now there were seven brothers, the first took a wife, and dying, left no children. The second took her, and died, neither did he leave any children and the third likewise, and the seventh had her, and left no children, last the woman died also. In the resurrection when they shall rise, whose wife shall she be? For the seven had her to wife."

Yahshua answering said to them, "You err, because you do not know the Scriptures, neither the power of Yahweh? For when they rise from the dead, they neither marry, nor are given in marriage, but are as the angels which are in Heaven. And as touching the dead, that they rise have you not read in the book of Moses, how in the bush Yahweh spoke to him, saying, 'I am the God of Abraham, the God of Isaac, and the God of Jacob?' He is not the God of the dead, but the God of the living. You therefore greatly err."

Then certain of the Scribes answering said, Master you have well said. And after that they dared not ask Him any more questions. But when the Pharisees heard that He put the Sadducees to silence, they were gathered together, one of them, a lawyer, asked tempting Him, saying, "Master, which is the greatest commandment in the Law?"

Yahshua answered him saying, "The first of all the commandments is, 'Hear, O Israel, Yahweh is our God, Yahweh is one. You shall love Yahweh your God with all your heart, with all your soul, with your entire mind and with all your strength.' This is the first and greatest commandment."

"And the second is like it, 'You shall love your neighbor as you love yourself.' There is no other commandment greater than these two. On these two commandments hang all the law and the prophets,"

The Scribe said to Him, "Well said Master, you have said the truth, for there is one God, and there is no other than He and to love Him with all the heart, with all the understanding, with all the soul, and with all your strength, and to love your neighbor as you love yourself, is more than all the whole burnt offerings and sacrifices."

When Yahshua saw that he answered discreetly, He said to him, "You are not far from the Kingdom of Yahweh." No man after that dared to ask Him anymore questions. Yahshua answered as He taught in the Temple, "Why do the Scribes say that the Messiah is the son of David? For David himself said by the Holy Spirit, 'The Lord said to my Lord, 'Sit on my right hand until I make your enemies your footstool.'"

"David calls Him Lord, and how is He his son?" No man was able to answer Him a word. The common people heard Him gladly. Then Yahshua spoke to the multitude, and to His disciples, saying, "The Scribes and the Pharisees sit in Moses' seat, whatever they bid you, observe and do, but do not after their works, for they say and do not. They bind heavy burdens and grievous to be borne, and lay them on men's shoulders, but they will not move them with one of their fingers."

"They do their works to be seen of men, they make broad their phylacteries, and enlarge the borders of their garments, they love the uppermost rooms at feasts, and the chief seats in their synagogues, to be greeted in the markets, and to be called of men, Rabbi, Rabbi. But do not be called

Rabbi, for one is your Master, the Messiah, and you are all brethren."

"Call no man your father on the earth, for one is your Father, who is in Heaven. Do not be called master, for one is your master, the Messiah." He that is greatest among you shall be your servant. Whoever shall exalt himself shall be abased, and he that shall humble himself shall be exalted."

"Woe to you Scribes and Pharisees, hypocrites, you shut up the Kingdom of Heaven against men, for you neither go in, neither suffer them that are entering to go in."

"Woe to you Scribes and Pharisees, you hypocrites! For you devour widows' houses and for pretenses make long prayer, therefore you will receive the greater damnation."

"Woe to you Scribes and Pharisees, you hypocrites! For you compass sea and land to make one proselyte, and when he is made, you make him twofold more the child of hell than yourselves."

"Woe to you, blind guides, which say, 'Whoever shall swear by the Temple, it is nothing, but whoever shall swear by the gold of the Temple, he is debtor!' Fools and blind, for which is greater the gold, or the Temple that sanctifies the gold?"

"Whoever shall swear by the altar, it is nothing, but whoever swears by the gift that is upon it, he is guilty. Fools and blind, for which is greater the gift, or the altar that sanctifies the gift? Whoever shall swear by the altar, swears by it, and by all things thereon. Whoever shall swear by the Temple, swears by it, and by Him that dwells therein. He that shall swear by Heaven swears by the Throne of Yahweh and by Him that sits thereon."

"Woe to you Scribes and Pharisees hypocrites! You pay tithe of mint and anise and cumin, and have omitted the weightier matters of the law, judgment, mercy, and faith, these you should have done, and not to leave the other undone."

"Blind guides who strain at a gnat and swallow a camel. Woe to you Scribes and Pharisees hypocrites! You make clean the outside of the cup and of the platter, but within they are full of extortion and excess. Blind Pharisees cleanse first that within the cup and platter, that the outside of them may be clean also."

"Woe to you Scribes and Pharisees hypocrites! You are like whited sepulchers which indeed appear beautiful outward, but are within full of dead bones and of all uncleanness. Even so you also outwardly appear righteous to men, but within you are full of hypocrisy and wickedness."

"Woe to you Scribes and Pharisees hypocrites! Because you build the tombs of the prophets, and garnish the sepulchers of the righteous, and say, 'If we had been in the days of our fathers, we would not have been partakers with them in the blood of the prophets.'"

"Wherefore you are witnesses against yourselves, that you are the children of them which killed the prophets. Fill up then the measure of your fathers. Serpents, generation of vipers, how can you escape the damnation of hell?"

"Wherefore, behold, I send to you prophets, and wise men, and Scribes, and of them you shall kill and crucify, and of them shall you scourge in your synagogues, and persecute from city to city, that upon you may come all the righteous blood shed upon the earth, from the blood of righteous Abel to the blood of Zechariah, son of Berechiah, whom you slew between the Temple and the altar. Verily I say to you, all these things shall come upon this generation."

"O Jerusalem, Jerusalem that kills the prophets, and stones them which are sent to you, how often I would have gathered your children together, even as a hen gathers her chickens under her wings, and you would not! Behold, your house is left to you desolate."

"I say to you, you shall not see me henceforth, until you shall say, 'Blessed is He that comes in the Name of Yahweh."

In the morning, as they passed by, they saw the fig tree dried up from the roots. Peter calling to remembrance said, "Master, behold, the fig tree which you cursed has withered away." Yahshua answering said to them, "Have faith in Yahweh. Verily I say to you, that whoever shall say to this mountain, 'Be removed, and be cast into the sea,' and shall not doubt in his heart, but shall believe that those things which he says shall come to pass, he shall have whatever he says."

"Therefore I say to you, 'Whatever things you desire, whatever you pray, believe that you will receive and you shall have it. When you stand praying, forgive if you have anything against anyone, that your Father also who is in Heaven may forgive you your trespasses. But if you do not forgive, neither will your Father who is in Heaven forgive you your trespasses."

Yahshua sat over against the treasury, and beheld how the people cast money into the treasury, and how many that were rich cast in much. There came a certain poor widow, and she threw in two mites, which make a farthing. He called His disciples together and said to them, "Verily I say to you that this poor widow has cast more in than all they who have cast into the treasury, for all did cast in of their abundance, but she of her want did cast in all that she had, all her living."

But even though He had done so many miracles before the Chief Priests and the Pharisees, yet they did not believe on him, that the saying of Isaiah the prophet might be fulfilled, which he spoke, "Lord, who has believed our report, and to whom has the arm of the Lord been revealed?" Therefore they could not believe, because Isaiah had said, "He has blinded their eyes, and hardened their hearts, that they should not see with their eyes, nor understand with their hearts, and be converted, and I should heal them."

These things said Isaiah, when he saw His glory, and spoke of Him. Nevertheless, among the Chief Rulers many believed on Him, but because of the Pharisees they did not confess, lest they should be put out of the synagogue, for they loved the praise of men more than the praise of Yahweh.

Yahshua cried and said, "He that believes on me, believes not on me, but on Him that sent me, and he that sees me sees Him that sent me. I am come a light into the world, that whoever believes on me shall not abide in darkness."

"If any man hear my words, and believes not, I judge him, the Word that I have spoken, the same shall judge him in the last day. I have not spoken of myself, but the Father who sent me. He gave me a commandment, what I should say, and what I should speak. And I know that His commandment is life everlasting. Whatever, I speak therefore, even as the Father said to me, so I speak."

It came to pass, when Yahshua had finished all these sayings, He said to His disciples, "You know that after two days is the Passover, and the Son of Man is betrayed to be crucified."

CHAPTER IX

The Chief Priests, Scribes, and the Elders of the people assembled together at the palace of the High Priest, who was called Caiaphas, and consulted how they might take Him by subtlety and kill Him. But they said, "Not on the Feast of the Passover, lest there be an uproar of the people," for they feared the people.

Then Satan entered into Judas, surnamed Iscariot, being of the number of the twelve, and he went his way, and communed with the Chief Priests and Captains, how he might betray Yahshua to them, and said, "What will you give me, and I will deliver Him to you?" When they heard this they were glad, and they covenanted with him thirty pieces of silver. From that time Judas sought opportunity to betray Him.

When Yahshua went out of the Temple, one of His disciples said to Him, "Master, see what manner of stones and buildings." Yahshua said to them, "Do you not see all these things? Verily I say to you, there shall not be left here one stone upon another that shall not be thrown down."

As He sat upon the Mount of Olives, over against the Temple, Peter, John and Andrew asked Him privately, "Tell us when these things shall be? What is the sign when all these things shall be fulfilled?"

Yahshua answering them began to say, "Take heed lest any deceive you, for many shall come in my Name, saying, I am Messiah, and shall deceive many. When you hear of wars and rumors of wars, be not troubled, for these things must be, but the end is not yet."

"Nation shall rise against nation, and kingdom against kingdom, and there shall be great earthquakes in divers places, and there shall be famines and pestilences, and fearful sights and great signs shall there be from heaven. But take heed to yourselves, because before all these happen, they shall lay their hands on you, and deliver you up to be afflicted, and they shall kill you, and you shall be hated of all nations for my Name's sake."

"They shall deliver you up to councils and in the synagogues you shall be beaten, and cast into prison and you shall be brought before rulers and kings for my sake, for a testimony against them."

"Then shall many be offended, and shall betray one another, and shall hate one another. Many false prophets shall arise, and shall deceive many, because iniquity shall abound, the love of many shall wax cold. He that shall endure to the end, the same shall be saved."

"This gospel of the Kingdom shall be preached in the entire world for a witness to all nations, and then shall the end come. When they shall lead, and deliver you up, take no thought beforehand what you shall speak, neither premeditate, but whatever shall be given you in that hour, that speak, for it is not you that speaks, but the Holy Spirit. Settle it in your heart, not to mediate before what you shall answer, for I will give you a mouth and wisdom, which all your adversaries shall not be able to gain say nor resist."

"You shall be betrayed by your parents, your brethren, your kinsfolk, and your friends, and many of you shall they cause to be put to death. You shall be hated of all for my Name's sake. But there shall not a hair of your head perish. In your patience possess your souls. He that shall endure to the end, the same shall be saved."

"When you shall see the abomination of desolation that makes desolate, spoken of by Daniel the prophet, standing where it ought not, (whoso readeth, let him understand), and when you shall see Jerusalem compassed with armies, then know that the desolation thereof is nigh, Let them which are in Judea flee to the mountains, and let them which are in the midst of it depart out of the it, and let not them that are in the countries enter there into."

"Let him which is on the housetop not come down to take anything out of his house, and let him that is in the field not turn back again to take up his garment, and woe to them that are with child, and to them that give suck in those days!"

"Pray that your flight be not in the winter, neither on the Sabbath. For these will be the days of vengeance that all things which are written may be fulfilled, and there shall be great distress in the land, and wrath upon this people, for then shall be great tribulation, such as was not since the beginning of the world to this time, no, nor ever shall be."

"They shall fall by the edge of the sword, and shall be led away captive into all nations, and Jerusalem shall be trodden down by the Gentiles, until the times of the Gentiles be fulfilled."

"Except those days should be shortened, there should no flesh be saved, but for the elect's sake those days shall be shortened. If any man shall say to you, lo, here is the Messiah, or, lo, there, believe it not. For false messiahs and false prophets shall arise, and shall show signs and wonders, to seduce, if possible, even the very elect."

"Behold, I have told you before, that if they shall say to you, 'Behold, he's in the desert.' Go not forth. 'Behold, in the secret chambers.' Believe it not. As the lightening comes out of the east, and shines even to the west, so also shall the coming of the Son of Man be."

"Wherever the carcass is, there will the eagles be gathered together. Immediately after the tribulation of those days the sun shall be darkened, the moon shall not give her light, and the stars shall fall from heaven, and the powers of the heavens shall be shaken, and upon the earth distress of nations, with perplexity, the sea and the waves roaring, men's hearts failing them for fear, and looking after those things which are coming on the earth, for the powers of heaven shall be shaken."

"When these things begin to come to pass, then look up, lift up your heads, for your redemption draws nigh, and then shall appear the sign of the Son of Man in heaven, and then shall all the tribes of the earth mourn. They shall see the Son of Man coming in the clouds of heaven with power and great glory."

"And then He shall send His angels with a great sound of the trumpet, and they shall gather together His elect from the four winds, from the uttermost part of the earth to the uttermost part of heaven."

"Now learn a parable of the fig tree, when her branch is yet tender, and puts forth leaves, you know that summer is near, so you in like manner, when you shall see these things come to pass, know that the kingdom of Yahweh is nigh at hand, even at the door. Verily I say to you, this generation shall not pass away, until all these things will be fulfilled. Heaven and earth shall pass away but my words shall not pass away. But of that day and hour no man knows, no, not the angels which are in heaven, neither the Son, but the Father only."

"Take heed, watch and pray, for you do not know when the time will be. Take heed to yourselves, lest at any time your hearts are overcharged with surfeiting drunkenness and the cares of this life, and that day come upon you unawares. As a snare it shall come on all them that dwell on the face of the whole earth."

"Watch and always pray that you may be accounted worthy to escape all these things that shall come to pass, and to stand before the Son of Man. As the days of Noah, so shall the coming of the Son of Man be. As in the days that were before the flood they were eating and drinking, marrying and giving in marriage, until the day Noah entered into the ark, and knew not until the flood came, and took them all away, so also shall the coming of the Son of Man be."

"I tell you, in that night there shall be two in one bed, the one shall be taken, and the other shall be left. There shall be two in the field, the one shall be taken, and the other left. Two will be grinding at the mill, the one shall be taken, and the other left."

"Watch therefore, for you will not know what hour the Lord will come. But know this that if the Goodman of the house had known in what watch the thief would come, he would have watched, and would not have suffered his house to be broken up. Therefore be also ready, for in such an hour as you think not the Son of Man comes."

"As a man taking a far journey that left his house, and gave authority to his servants, and assigned to every man his work, and commanded the porter to watch. Watch therefore, for you do not know when the master of the house comes, at even, or at midnight, or at the cock crowing, or in the morning, lest coming suddenly he find you sleeping."

Yahshua spoke a parable to them that men ought always to pray and not to faint, saying, "There was in a city a judge, who did not fear God, neither regarded man. And there was a widow in that city, and she came unto him, crying, 'Avenge me of mine adversary.' And he would not for a while, but afterward he said within himself, 'Though I fear not God, nor regard man, yet because this widow troubles me, I will avenge her, lest by her continual coming she weary me.'"

Yahshua said, "Hear what the unjust judge says. Shall not Yahweh avenge His own elect, which cry day and night to Him, though He bears long with them? I tell you that He will avenge them speedily. Nevertheless when the Son of Man comes, shall He find faith on earth?"

He spoke this parable to certain of those who trusted in themselves that they were righteous, and despised others." Two men went up into the Temple to pray, the one a Pharisee, and the other a Publican. The Pharisee stood and prayed thus with himself, 'God, I thank you, that I am not as other men, extortionist, unjust, adulterers, or even as this Publican. I fast twice in the week. I give tithes of all that I possess.'"

"The Publican, standing afar off, would not lift up so much as his eyes unto heaven, but smote upon his breast, saying, 'God, be merciful to me a sinner.' I tell you, this man went down to his house justified than the other. Everyone that exalts himself shall be abased, and he that humbles himself shall be exalted."

"Then shall the Kingdom of Heaven be likened to ten virgins, who took their lamps, and went forth to meet the bridegroom. Five of them were wise, and five foolish. They that were foolish took their lamps, and took no oil with them. But the wise took oil in their vessels with their lamps. While the bridegroom tarried, they all slumbered and slept. At midnight there was a cry made, 'Behold, the bridegroom comes. Go out to meet him.' The foolish said to the wise, 'Give us of your oil, for our lamps have gone out.' But the wise answered saying, 'Not so, lest there be not enough for us and you. But go rather to them that sell and buy for your selves.'

"While they went to buy, the bridegroom came, and they that were ready went in with him to the marriage, and the door was shut. Afterward the other virgins also came, saying, 'Lord. Lord, open to us.' But he answered and said, 'Verily I say to you, I do not know you.' Watch therefore, for you do not know the day or the hour wherein the Son of Man comes."

"As a man traveling into a far country called his own servants, and delivered to them his goods. To one he gave five talents, to another two, and to another one, to every man according to his ability and straightway took his journey. He that had received the five talents went and traded with the same, and made another five talents."

"Likewise he that had two, he also gained other two, but he that had received one went and dug in the earth, and hid his lord's money. After a long time the lord of those servants came and reckoned with them."

"He that had received five talents came and brought another five talents, 'Behold, I have gained beside these five talents more,' His lord said to him, 'Well done good and faithful servant, you have been faithful over a few things, I will make you ruler over many things enter into the joy of your lord.'"

"He also that had received two talents came and said, 'Lord, you delivered to me two talents, behold, I have gained two other talents beside them'. His lord said to him, 'Well done, good and faithful servant, you have been faithful over a few things, I will make you ruler over many things, enter into the joy of your lord.'"

"Then he who had received the one talent came and said, 'Lord, I know that you are a hard man, reaping where you have not sown, and gathering where you have not strewed. I was afraid, and went and hid your talent in the earth, lo, you have what is yours.'"

"His lord answered and said to him, 'Wicked and slothful servant. You knew that I reap where I have not strewed. You should have put my money to the exchangers, and at my coming I should have received mine own with interest."

"'Take the talent from him and give it to him who has ten talents. To everyone that has shall be given, and he shall have in abundance, but from him that has not it shall be taken away even that which he has. Cast the unprofitable servant into outer darkness. There shall be weeping and gnashing of teeth.'"

Yahshua said to them, "Verily I say to you, the Kingdom of Heaven is like to a man, a householder, who went out early in the morning to hire laborers into his vineyard. When he had agreed with the laborers for a penny a day, he sent them into his vineyard."

"About the third hour he went out, and saw others standing idle in the market place and said to them, 'Go also into the vineyard, and whatever is right I will give you.' Again about the sixth and ninth hours he went out, and did likewise."

"About the eleventh hour he went out, and found others standing idle, and said to them, 'Why do you stand here all day idle?' They said to him, 'Because no man has hired us.' He said to them 'Go also into the vineyard and whatever is right you will receive.'"

"When it was evening the lord of the vineyard said to his steward, 'Call the laborers, and give them their hire, beginning from the last to the first.' When they came that were hired about the eleventh hour, they received everyman a penny. But when the first came, they supposed that they should have received more, and they likewise received every man a penny."

"When they had received they murmured against the Goodman of the house saying, 'These last have wrought one hour, and you have made them equal to us, who have borne the burden and heat of the day,' The Goodman of the house answered one of them and said, 'Friend, I do you no wrong. Did you not agree with me for a penny? Take your wages and go your way, I will give to this last, even as to you. Is it not lawful for me to do what I will with what is mine? So the last shall be first, and the first last, for many are called, but few are chosen."

"Which of you having a servant plowing or feeding cattle will say to him by and by, when he comes from the field, 'Go and sit down to meat?' And will not rather say to him, 'Make ready wherewith I may sup, and gird yourself and serve me until I have eaten and drunken, and afterward you shalt eat and drink?'"

"Does he thank that servant because he did the things that were commanded him? I think not. So likewise, when you shall have done all those things which are commanded of you say, 'We are unprofitable servants, we have only done that which was our duty to do.'"

CHAPTER X

"Yahweh continued to speak saying, "Who then is a faithful and wise servant, whom his lord has made ruler over his household, to give them meat in due season? Blessed be that servant, whom his lord when he comes shall find so doing. Verily I say to you, that he shall make him ruler over all his goods."

"But if that evil servant shall say in his heart, 'My lord delays his coming, and shall begin to smite fellow servants, and to eat and drink with the drunken, the lord of that servant shall come in a day when he looks not, and in an hour that he is not aware of, and shall cut him asunder, and appoint his portion with the hypocrites. There shall be weeping and gnashing of teeth. What I say to you, I say to all, 'Watch.'"

"When the Son of Man shall come in His glory, and all the holy angels with Him, then shall He sit upon the Throne of His glory, and before Him shall be gathered all nations, and He shall separate them one from another as a shepherd divides the sheep from the goats. He shall set the sheep on His right hand, and the goats on the left."

"Then shall the King say to them on His right hand, 'Come blessed of my Father, inherit the Kingdom prepared for you from the foundation of the world, for I was hungry and you gave me meat. I was thirsty, and you gave me drink. I was a stranger, and you took me in, naked, and you clothed me. I was sick and you visited me. I was in prison, and you came to me.'"

"Then shall the righteous answer Him, saying, 'Lord, when were you a stranger, and we took you in? Or naked, and we clothed? Or when did we see you sick, or in prison and came to you?' The King shall answer and say to them, 'Verily I say to you, inasmuch as you have done it to one of the least of these my brethren, you have done it to me.'"

"Then shall He say also to them on the left hand, 'Depart from me, you cursed into everlasting fire, prepared for the devil and his angels. I was hungry, and you gave me no meat. I was thirsty, and you gave me no drink. I was a stranger, and you did not take me in, naked, and you did not clothe me, sick, and in prison, and you did not visit me."

"Then they answered Him, saying, 'Lord, when did we see you hungry, or athirst, or a stranger, or naked, or sick, or in prison, and did not minister to you?' Then shall He answer them saying,

'Verily I say to you, inasmuch as you did not do it to one of the least of these, you did it not to me.' And these shall go away into everlasting punishment and the righteous into life eternal."

Now on the first days of preparation for the Feast of Unleavened Bread the disciples came to Yahshua, saying to Him, "Where will you have us prepare for the Passover?" He sent Peter and John saying, "When you have entered into the city, there you will see a man bearing a pitcher of water, follow him into the house where he enters."

"You will say to the Goodman of the house, 'The Master has said, 'My time is at hand, I will keep the Passover with my disciples at your house.' And he will show you a large upper room furnished. There make ready. They went, and found as He had said to them, and they made ready the Passover.

In the evening He came with the twelve. And when the hour had come, He sat down, and the twelve apostles with Him. He said to them, "With desire I have desired to keep this Passover with you. I say to you, I will not eat thereof, until it be fulfilled in the Kingdom of Yahweh."

He took bread, gave thanks, broke it and gave it to then saying, "This is my body which is given for you, do this in remembrance of me." Likewise also after supper, He took the cup, and gave thanks, and said, "Take this, and divide it among yourselves, for I say to you, I will not drink of the fruit of the vine until the Kingdom of Yahweh shall come. This cup is the New testament in my blood which is shed for many for the remission of sins."

There was a strife among them, which of them should be accounted the greatest and He said to them, "The kings of the Gentiles exercise lordship over them, and they that exercise authority on them are called benefactors. But you shall not be so. He that is greatest among you, let him be as the younger, and he that is chief, as he that serves."

"You are they who have continued with me in my temptations. I appoint to you a kingdom, as my Father has appointed to me that you may eat and drink at my table in my Kingdom, and sit on thrones judging the twelve tribes of Israel."

Now before the Feast of the Passover, when Yahshua knew that His hour had come that He would depart out of this world and go to the Father, having loved His own which were in the world, He loved them to the end.

After supper being ended the devil having now put into the heart of Judas Iscariot, Simon's son, to betray Him. Yahshua knowing that the Father had given all things into His hands, and that

He had come from Yahweh, and went to Yahweh, He rose from supper and laid aside His garments, and took a towel, and girded Himself.

After that He poured water into a basin and began to wash the disciple's feet, and to wipe them with the towel wherewith He was girded. When He came to Simon Peter, Peter said to Him, "Lord, do you wash my feet?" Yahshua answered and said to him, "What I do you do not know now, but you will know hereafter." Peter said to Him, "You shall never wash my feet." Yahshua answered him, "If I do not wash your feet, you will have no part with me." Simon Peter said to Him, 'Lord, not my feet only, but also my hands and my head."

Yahshua said to him, "He that is washed needs not save to wash feet, but is clean every whit, and you are clean, but not all." For He knew who should betray Him, therefore He said, "You are not all clean."

After He had washed their feet and had taken His garments, and had set down again, He said to them, "Know you what I have done to you? You call me Master and Lord, and you say well, for I am. If I then, Lord and Master, have washed your feet, you also ought to wash one another's feet. I have given you an example that you should do as I have done to you."

"Verily, verily, I say to you, the servant is not greater than his lord, neither he that is sent greater than he that sent him. If you know these things happy are you if you do them. I speak not of you all, I know whom I have chosen, but that the Scripture may be fulfilled, 'He that eats bread with me has lifted up his heel against me.'"

"Now I tell you before it comes, that, when it has come to pass you may believe that I am. Verily, verily, I say to you, he that receives whoever I send receives me, and he that receives me receives Him that sent me."

"When Yahshua had thus said, He was troubled in His spirit, and testified, saying, "Verily, verily, I say to you that one of you who eat with me will betray me." The disciples looked on one another, and were exceeding sorrowful, and every one of them began to say to Him, "Lord, is it I?"

Now there was leaning on Yahshua's bosom one of His disciples, whom Yahshua loved. Simon Peter beckoned to him, that he should ask who it would be of whom He spoke. He that lay on Yahshua's breast said to Him, "Lord, who is it?" Yahshua answered, "It is he, to whom I shall give a sop when I have dipped, is the same one who will betray me."

"The Son of Man goes as it is written of Him, but woe to that man by whom the Son of man is betrayed! It had been good for that man if he had not been born." When He had dipped the sop He gave it to Judas Iscariot, the son of Simon.

After the sop Satan entered into him. Then Judas, who betrayed Him, answered and said, "Master, is it I?" He said to him, "You have said. That you must do, do quickly."

Now no man at the table knew for what intent He spoke this to him. Some thought because Judas had the bag, that Yahshua had said to him, "Buy that we have need of against the Feast." Or that he would give something to the poor. He then, having received the sop, went out immediately, and it was night.

When he had gone out, Yahshua said, "Now is the Son of Man glorified, and Yahweh is glorified in Him. If Yahshua be glorified in Him, Yahweh shall also glorify Him in Himself, and shall straightway glorify Him."

"Little children yet a little while will I be with you. You will seek me, and as I said to the Chief Priests and Pharisees, where I go you cannot come, so now a new commandment I give to you, that you love one another as I have loved you, that you may also love one another. By this shall all men know that you are my disciples, if you have love one for another."

Simon Peter said to Him, "Lord, where do you go?" Yahshua answered him, "Where I go you cannot follow now, but you will follow afterwards." Peter said to Him, "Lord, why cannot I follow you now? I will lay down my life for your sake."

The Lord said, "Simon, Simon, behold, Satan has desired you that he may sift you as wheat. But I have prayed for you, that your faith will not fail. And when you are converted, strengthen your brethren." Simon said to Him, "Lord, I am ready to go with you, both into prison, and to death."

Yahshua said to them, "When I sent you without purse, and script, and shoes, did you lack anything?" They answered, "Nothing." Then He said to them, "But now, he that has a purse, let him take, and likewise script, and he that has no sword, let him sell his garment, and buy one. For I say to you, that this that is written must yet be accomplished in me, 'And He was reckoned among the transgressors,' for the things concerning me have an end." They said, "Behold Lord here is two swords." He said to them, "It is enough."

And when they had sung a hymn, they went out into the Mount of Olives. Yahshua said to them, "All you will be offended because of me this night, for it is written: 'I will smite the shepherd, and the sheep shall be scattered.' But after I am raised I will go before you into Galilee."

But Peter said to Him, "Although all shall be offended, yet not I." Yahshua said to him, "Verily I say to you that this day, in this night, before the cock crow twice, you will deny me thrice." But Peter spoke the more vehemently, "If I should die with you, I will not deny you in any wise." They all said the same thing.

Yahshua said to them, "Let not your heart be troubled you believe in Yahweh, believe also in me, in my Father's house are many mansions, if not, I would have told you. I go to prepare a place for you. If I go and prepare a place for you, I will come again, and receive you to myself, that where I am, you may be also. And where I go you know, and the way you know."

Thomas saith to Him, "Lord, we know not where you go, and how can we know the way?" Yahshua said to him, "I am the way, the truth, and the life, no man comes to the Father, but by me. If you had known me you should have known my Father also, and from henceforth you know Him, and have seen Him."

Philip said to Him, "Lord, show us the Father, and it suffices us." Yahshua said to him,"

Have I been so long time with you, and yet hast you not known me Philip? He that has seen me has seen the Father, and how do you, 'Show us the Father?' Do you not believe that I am in the Father, and the Father is in me?"

"The words that I speak to you I speak not of myself, but the Father that dwells in me, He does the works. Believe me that I am in the Father, and the Father is in me, or else believe me for the very works' sake."

"Verily, verily, I say to you, 'He that believe on me, the works that I do shall He also do and greater works than these shall he do, because I go to my Father. And whatever you shall ask in my Name that will I do, that the Father may be glorified in the Son."

"If you ask anything in my Name, I will do it. If you love me, keep my commandments. And I will pray the Father, and He will give you another Comforter that He may abide with you forever, the Spirit of Truth, whom the world cannot receive, because it cannot see the Spirit, neither knows it, but you know it, for it dwells with you, and shall be in you."

"I will not leave you comfortless, I will come to you. Yet a little while, and the world sees me no more, but you see me, because I live, you will live also. At that day you will know that I am in my Father, and you are in me, and I am in you. He that has my commandments, and keeps them, he it is that loves me, and he that loves me shall be loved of my Father, and I will love him, and will manifest myself to him."

Judas said to Him, not Iscariot, "Lord, how is it that you will manifest yourself to us, and not to the world?" Yahshua answered and said to him, "If a man love me he will keep my words, and my Father will love him, and we will come to him. He that loves me not, keeps not my sayings, and the word which you hear is not mine, but my Father's, who sent me."

"These things have I spoken to you, being present with you. But the Comforter, the Holy Spirit, which the Father will send in my Name, He will teach you all things, and bring all things to your remembrance whatever I have said to you."

" Peace, I leave with you, my peace I give to you, not as the world gives, give I to you. Let not your heart be troubled, neither let it be afraid. You have heard how I said to you, I go away, and I will come to you. If you loved me, you would rejoice, because I said, 'I go to my Father,' for my Father is greater than I am."

"Now I have told you before it come to pass, that, when it has come to pass, you might believe. Hereafter I will not talk much with you, for the prince of this world comes, and has nothing in me. But that the world may know that I love my Father, and as the Father gave me commandment, even so I do."

"I am the true vine, and my Father is the husbandman. Every branch in me that bears not fruit He takes away, and every branch that bears fruit, He purges it, that it may bring forth more fruit. Now ye are clean through the word which I have spoken to you. Abide in me, and I in you. As the branch cannot bear fruit of itself, except it abides in the vine, no more can you, except you abide in me."

"I am the vine, you are the branches. He that abides in me, and I in him, the same brings forth much fruit, for without me you can do nothing. If a man does not abide in me, he is cast forth as a branch, and is withered, and men gather them, and cast them into the fire, and they are burned. If you abide in me, and my words abide in you, you will ask what you will, and it will be done to you."

"Herein is My Father glorified, that you bear much fruit, so shall you be my disciples. As the Father has loved me, so have I loved you, continue in my love. If you keep my commandments, you will abide in my love, even as I have kept my Father's commandments, and abide in His love."

"These things have I spoken to you that my joy might remain in you, and your joy might be full. This is my commandment, that you love one another as I have loved you. Greater love has no man than this that a man lay down his life for his friends. You are my friends, if you do whatever I command you."

Henceforth I do not call you servants, for the servant knows not what his lord does, but I have called you friends, for all things that I have heard of my Father I have made known to you. You have not chosen me, but I have chosen you, and ordained you, that you should go and bring forth fruit, and your fruit should remain, that whatever you shall ask of my Father in my Name, He may give it to you."

"These things I command you, that you love one another. If the world hates you, you know that it hated me before you. If you were of the world, the world would love its own but because you are not of the world, I have chosen you out of the world, therefore the world hates you."

"Remember the word that I said to you, the servant is not greater than his lord. If they have persecuted me, they will also persecute you, if they have kept my saying, they will keep yours also, but all these things will they do to you for my Name's sake, because they know not Him that sent me."

"If I had not come and spoken to them, they would not have had sin, but now they have no cloak for their sin. He that hates me hates my Father also. If I had not done among them the works which none other man did, they would not have had sin, but now they have both seen and hated both me and my Father."

"That the word might be fulfilled that is written in their law, 'They hated me without cause.' But the Comforter will come, which I will send to you from the Father, the Spirit of Truth, which proceeds from the Father, it will testify of me, and you also will bear witness, because you have been with me from the beginning."

"These things have I spoken to you, that you should not be offended. They will put you out of the synagogues yea the time will come, that whoever kills you will think that he does God service. These things they will do to you, because they have not known the Father, or me."

"These things I have told you so that when the time comes, you may remember that I told you about them. These things I did not say to you at the beginning, because I was with you. But now I go my way to Him that sent me and none of you asks me. 'Where do you go?'"

"Because I have said these things to you, sorrow has filled your heart. Nevertheless I tell you the truth it is expedient for you that I go away, for if I do not go away, the Comforter will not come to you. But if I depart, I will send it to you."

"When the Spirit of Truth has come, it will reprove the world of sin, and of righteousness, and of judgment: Of sin, because they believe not on me; of righteousness, because I go to my Father, and you will see me no more; of judgment, because the prince of this world is judged."

"I have many things yet to say to you, but you cannot bear them now. Howbeit when the Spirit of Truth has come, it will guide you into all truth, for it will not speak of itself. Whatever it hears it shall speak, and the Spirit will show you things to come. It will glorify me, for the Spirit will receive of mine and shall show it to you. All things that the Father has are mine, therefore I said, that it shall take of what is mine and show it to you."

"A little while, and you will not see me, and again, a little while, and you will see me, because I go to the Father." His disciples spoke among themselves saying, "What is this that He says to us, 'A little while, and you will not see me, and again, a little while, and you will see me,' and 'Because I go to my Father.' They said therefore, "What is this that He says, 'A little while?' We cannot understand what He says."

Now Yahshua knew that they were desirous to ask Him, and said to them, "Do you inquire among yourselves of that which I said, 'A little while, and you will not see me, and again, a little while, and you shall see me?'"

"Verily, verily, I say to you, that you will weep and lament, but the world will rejoice, and you will be sorrowful, but your sorrow will be turned into joy."

"A woman when she is in travail has sorrow, because her hour has come, but as soon as she is delivered of the child, she remembers no more the anguish, for joy that a man is born into the world. You now have sorrow, but I will see you again, and your heart will rejoice, and your joy no man can take it from you."

"In that day you will ask nothing. Verily, verily, I say to you, 'Whatever you shall ask the Father in my Name, He will give you. Hitherto you have asked nothing in my Name. Ask, and you shall receive, that your joy may be full."

"These things have I spoken to you in proverbs, but the time comes, when I will no more speak to you in proverbs, but I will show you plainly of the Father."

"At that day you shall ask in my Name, and I say not to you, that I will pray the Father for you, for the Father Himself loves you, because you have loved me, and have believed that I came out from Yahweh."

"I came forth from the Father, and am come into the world again I leave the world, and go to the Father." His disciples said to Him, "Lo, now you speak plainly, and speak no proverb. Now are we sure that you know all things, and need not that any man should ask you. By this we believe that you came forth from Yahweh."

Yahshua answered them, "Do you now believe? Behold, the hour comes, yea, has now come, that you shall be scattered, every man to his own, and shall leave me alone, and yet I am not alone, because the Father is with me."

"These things I have spoken to you, that in me you might have peace. In the world you will have tribulation, but be of good cheer, I have overcome the world."

CHAPTER XI

They came to a place which was named Gethsemane, and He said to His disciples, "Sit here, while I pray." He took with Him Peter and the two sons of Zebedee, James and John, and began to be sore amazed, and to be very heavy, and said to them, "My soul is exceeding sorrowful to death. Wait here, and watch with me. Pray that you enter not into temptation."

He withdrew from them about a stone's cast, and kneeled down, and prayed, "Abba Father, all things are possible to You, if You are willing remove this cup from me, nevertheless, not my will but let Your will be done."

These words spoke Yahshua, and lifting up His eyes to heaven, and said, "Father, the hour is come, glorify Your Son, that Your Son also may glorify You, as You have given Him power over all flesh, that He should give eternal life to as many as You have given Him."

"This is life eternal, that they might know You the only true God, and Yahshua the Messiah, whom You have sent. I have glorified You on the earth I have finished the work which You gave me to do. And now, O Father, glorify me with Your own self with the glory which I had with You before the world was."

"I have manifested Your Name to the men who You gave me out of the world, Yours they were, and You gave them to me, and they have kept Your word. Now they have known that all things whatever You have given me are of You. I have given to them the words which You gave me, and they have received, and have known surely that I came from You, and they have believed that You did send me."

"I pray for them, I pray not for the world, but for them which You have given me, for they are Yours. All that are mine are Yours, and Yours are mine, and I am glorified in them. Now I am no more in the world, but these are in the world, and I come to You. Holy Father, keep through mine own Name those whom You have given me that they may be one, as We are one."

"While I was with them in the world, I kept them in Your Name. Those that You gave me I have kept, and none of them is lost, but the son of perdition, that the Scripture might be fulfilled."

"Now I come to You and these things I speak in the world, that they might have my joy fulfilled in themselves. I have given them Your word, and the world has hated them, because they are not of the world. I pray not that You should take them out of the world, but that You should keep them from the evil one."

"They are not of the world, even as I am not of the world. Sanctity them through Your truth, Your Word is the truth. As You have sent me into the world, even so have I also sent them into the world, for their sakes I sanctify myself, that they also might be sanctified through the truth."

"Neither pray I for these alone, but for them also which shall believe on me through their word, that they all may be one, as You, Father, are in me, and I am in You, that they also may be one in Us, that the world may believe that You have sent me."

"The glory which You gave me I have given to them that they may be one, even as We are One. I in them, and You in me, that they may be made perfect in one, and that the world may know that You have sent me, and has loved them, as You have loved me."

"Father, I will that they also, whom You have given me, may be with me where I am, that they may behold my glory, which You have given me, for You loved me before the foundation of the world."

"Righteous Father, the world has not known You, but I have known You, and these have known that You have sent me. And I have declared to them Your Name, and I will declare it, that the love wherewith You have loved me may be in them, and I in them."

An angel then came to Him from heaven, giving him strength. Being in agony He prayed more earnestly, and His sweat was as it were great drops of blood falling down to the ground. When He rose from prayer, and came to His disciples, He found them sleeping for sorrow, and said to Peter, "Simon, do you sleep? Could you not watch for one hour? Watch and pray, lest you enter into temptation. The spirit is willing, but the flesh is weak."

He went away again the second time, and prayed saying, "O my Father, if this cup may not pass away from me except I drink it, Your will be done." He came and found them asleep again, for their eyes were heavy. He left them, and went away again, and prayed the third time, saying the same words. Then He came to His disciples, and said to them, "Sleep on now, and take your rest, behold, the hour is at hand, and the Son of Man is betrayed into the hands of sinners."

When Yahshua had spoken these words, He went forth with His disciples over the brook Cedron, where there was a garden, into which He and His disciples entered. Judas, who betrayed Him, also knew the place, for Yahshua oft times resorted thither with His disciples.

Immediately, while He yet spoke, Judas, one of the twelve, and with him a great multitude with swords and staves, from the Chief Priests and the Scribes and the Elders, came thither with lanterns, torches and weapons. And Judas, who had betrayed Him had given them a token saying, "Whomever I shall kiss, the same is He, and lead Him away safely."

As soon as he had come, he went straightway to Him and said, "Master, Master" and kissed Him. Yahshua said to him, "Judas, do you betray the Son of Man with a kiss?" Yahshua, knowing all things that should come upon Him, went forth and said to them, "Whom do you seek?" They answered Him, "Yahshua of Nazareth." Yahshua said to them, "I am He."

Judas also which betrayed Him, stood with them. As soon then as He had said to them, "I am He, they went backward, and fell to the ground. He then asked them again, "Whom do you seek?" They said, "Yahshua of Nazareth." Yahshua answered, "I have told you that I am He. If you seek me, then let these go their way. That the saying might be fulfilled, 'Of them which You gave me I have lost none.'"

They laid their hands on Him, and took Him. When they which were about Him saw what would follow, they asked Him, "Lord, shall we smite them with the sword?" Simon Peter having a sword drew it, and smote the High Priest's servant, and cut off his right ear. The servant's name was Malchus.

Yahshua then said to Peter, "Put up your sword into the sheath, the cup which my Father has given me, shall I not drink it? All who take up the sword shall perish with the sword. Do you think that I cannot now pray to my Father, and He will presently give me more than twelve legions of angels? But how then shall the Scriptures be fulfilled, that thus it must be?"

In that same hour Yahshua said to the multitudes, "Have you come out as against a thief with swords and staves to take me? I sat daily with you teaching in the Temple, and you laid no hold on me."

All this was done, that the Scriptures of the prophets might be fulfilled. Then all the disciples forsook him and fled. There followed Him a certain young man, having a linen cloth cast about him, and the young men laid hold on him, and he left the linen cloth, and fled from them naked.

They that had laid hands on Him, bound Him and led Him away to Annas first, for he was the father-in-law to Caiaphas, who was High Priest that same year, and then to the High Priest, and with him were assembled all the Chief Priests and the Elders and the Scribes.

Now Caiaphas was he, who gave counsel that it was expedient that one man should die for the people. Peter followed Yahshua afar off, as did another disciple. That disciple was known to the High Priest and went in with Yahshua into the palace of the High Priest.

Peter stood outside the door. Then that other disciple went out, who was known of the High Priest, and spoke to her that kept the door, and brought Peter in who sat with the servants to see the end of the matter.

The damsel that kept the door said to Peter, "Aren't you also of this man's disciples?" He said, "I am not." The servants and officers, who had made a fire of coals, stood there for it was cold, and they warmed themselves by the fire. Peter stood with them, and warmed himself.

About the space of one hour after, a maid saw him and began to say to them that stood by, "This is one of them." But he denied it again. And a little while after they that stood by again said to

Peter, "Surely you are one of them, for you are a Galilean, and your speech agrees."

Peter began to curse and to swear, saying, "I do not know this man or of whom you speak." A second time the cock crew, and the Lord turned and looked upon Peter, and Peter called to mind the word that Yahshua had said to him, "Before the cock crows twice, you will deny me thrice." When Peter thought thereon, he wept bitterly.

Now the Chief Priests, and Elders and all, the Council, sought false witnesses against Yahshua to put Him to death, but even though many false witnesses came, they found none.

At last came two false witnesses, and said, "This man said, 'I am able to destroy the Temple of God, and to build it in three days.'" The High Priest arose, and said to Him, "You have nothing to answer to what these witnesses say against you?" But Yahshua held His peace and said nothing.

The men that held Yahshua mocked Him, and when they had blindfolded Him, they struck Him on the face, and asked Him, saying, "Prophesy who is it that smote you? And many other things blasphemously spoke they against him. The High Priest then asked Yahshua of His disciples, and of His doctrine.

Yahshua answered him, I spoke openly to the world, I always taught in the synagogue, and in the Temple, where the Chief Priests and the Pharisees always resort, and in secret I have said nothing. Why do you ask me? Ask them who heard what I have said to them, behold, they know what I said."

When He had spoken one of the officers who stood by struck Yahshua with the palm of his hand saying, "Do you dare to answer the High Priest so?" Yahshua answered him, "If I have spoken evil, bear witness of the evil, but if well, why do you smite me?"

As soon as it was day, the Elders of the people and the Chief Priests and the Scribes came together, and led him into their Council saying, "Are you the Messiah? Tell us." Yahshua said to them, "If I tell you, you will not believe, and if I also ask, you will not answer me, nor let go."

Again the High Priest asked Him, and said to him, "I adjure you by the living God, that you tell us whether you are the Messiah, the Son of God." Yahshua said to him, "As you have said, I am, nevertheless I say to you, hereafter you will see the Son of Man sitting on the right hand of power, and coming in the clouds of heaven."

The High Priest rent his clothes, saying, "He has spoken blasphemy, what further need have we of witnesses? Behold, now you have heard His blasphemy. What do you think?" They answered and said, "He is guilty of death." They all condemned Him to be guilty of death. Some of them began to spit in His face, and buffeted Him, and the servants did strike Him with the palms of their hands.

Then Judas, who had betrayed Him, when he saw that He was condemned, repented and brought again the thirty pieces of silver to the Chief Priests and Elders, saying, "I have sinned in that I have betrayed innocent blood." They said, "What is that to us. See to that."

Judas cast down the pieces of silver in the Temple, departed, and went and hanged himself. The Chief Priests took the thirty pieces of silver, and said, "It is not lawful for us to put them into the treasury, because it is the price of blood." They took counsel, and bought with them the potter's field, to bury strangers in. Wherefore that field is called, "The field of blood," to this day.

Then was fulfilled that which was spoken by Zechariah the prophet saying, "And they took the thirty pieces of silver, the price of Him that was valued, whom they of the children of Israel did value, and gave them for the potter's field, as the Lord appointed me."

And straightway the whole Council bound Yahshua, and led Him away and delivered Him to Pontius Pilate, the governor, and it was early and they themselves went not into the judgment hall, lest they should be defiled, but that they might eat the Passover.

Pilate went out to them, and said, "What accusation do you bring against this man?" They answered and said to him, "If He were not a malefactor we would not have delivered him up to you." Then Pilate said to them, "Take Him, and judge Him according to your law." The Chief Priests said to him, "It is not lawful for us to put any man to death." That the saying of Yahshua might be fulfilled, which He spoke, signifying what death He should die.

And they began to accuse Him, saying, "We found this man perverting the nation, and forbidding others to give tribute to Caesar, saying that He Himself is the Messiah, a King." Pilate asked Him saying, "Are you the King of the Jews?" Yahshua answered him and said, "You have said."

The Chief Priests accused Him of many things, but He answered nothing. And Pilate asked Him again, "Will you not answer? Behold how many things they witness." But Yahshua still answered nothing so that Pilate marveled. Then Pilate said to the Chief Priests and to the Rulers of the people, "I find no fault in this man."

And they were the more fierce, saying, "He stirs up the people, teaching throughout all Israel beginning from Galilee to this place." When Pilate heard of Galilee, he asked whether the man were a Galilean. As soon as he knew that He belonged to Herod's jurisdiction, he sent Him to Herod, who himself also was at Jerusalem at that time.

When Herod saw Yahshua, he was exceeding glad, for he was desirous to see Him of a long time, because he had heard many things about Him, and he hoped to have seen some miracle done by Him. Herod questioned with Him in many words, but He answered him nothing. The Chief Priests and Scribes stood and vehemently accused Him.

Herod with his men of war set Him at naught, mocked Him, arrayed Him in a gorgeous robe and sent Him again to Pilate. The same day Pilate and Herod were made friends together, for before they were at enmity between themselves.

When Pilate was set down on the judgment seat, his wife sent to him, saying, "Have nothing to do with that just man, for I have suffered many things this day in a dream because of Him."

Then Pilate entered into the judgment hall again, and called for Yahshua and said to Him, "Are you the King of the Jews?" Yahshua answered him, "Do you say this thing of yourself, or did others tell it of me?" Pilate answered, "Am I a Jew? Your own nation and the Chief Priests have delivered you to me. What have you done?"

Yahshua answered. "My Kingdom is not of this world. If my Kingdom were of this world, then would my servants fight, that I should not be delivered to the Chief Priests, but now my Kingdom is not from hence." Pilate said to Him, "Are you a king then?" Yahshua answered, "You say that I am a king. To this end was I born, and for this cause I came into the world, that I should bear witness to the truth. Everyone that is of the truth hears my voice."

Pilate said to Him, "What is truth?" When he had said this, he went out again to the Chief Priests and the Rulers of the people and said to them, "You have brought this man to me as one that perverts the people, and, behold, I, having examined Him before you, have found no fault in this man touching those things whereof you accuse Him."

"No nor did Herod for I sent you to him, and lo, nothing worthy of death is done to Him. I will therefore chastise Him, and release Him." (For of necessity he must release one to them at the Feast of the Passover).

They cried out all at once, saying, "Away with this man, and release to us Barabbas." (Who for certain sedition made in the city, and for murder, and was cast into prison). Pilate therefore, willing to release Yahshua spoke again to them. But they cried, saying, "Crucify Him, Crucify Him." The governor said, "Why, what evil has He done?"

But they cried out the more saying, "Let Him be crucified." When Pilate saw that he could prevail nothing, but rather a tumult was made, he took water, and washed his hands before the multitude, saying, "I am innocent of the blood of this just person, see to it."

And Pilate gave sentence that it should be as they required, and he released Barabbas to them. Then Pilate delivered Yahshua after he had Him scourged, to be crucified. The soldiers led Him away into the hall called Pretorium, and they call together the whole band. They stripped Him of His clothing and put on Him a scarlet robe and platted a crown of thorns, and put it about His head, and began to salute Him, "Hail, King of the Jews." They smote Him on the head with a reed, and spit upon Him, and bowing their knees worshipped Him.

Pilate therefore went forth again and said to them, "Behold I bring Him forth to you, that you may know that I find no fault in Him." Then Yahshua came forth wearing the crown of thorns, and a purple robe. Pilate said to them, "Behold the man!"

When the Chief Priests and the officers saw Him, they cried out, saying! "Crucify Him. Crucify Him."

Pilate said to them, "Take Him, and crucify Him, for I find no fault in Him," The Chief Priests answered him." We have a law, and by our law He ought to die, because He has made Himself the Son of God." When Pilate heard that saying, he was the more afraid, and went again into the judgment hall, and said to Yahshua, "Where are you from?"

But Yahshua gave him no answer. Then Pilate said to Him, "You will not speak to me? Don't you know that I have power to crucify you, and I have power to release you?" Yahshua answered, "You could have no power against me, except it were given you from above, but he that delivered me to you has the greater sin."

And from moment Pilate sought to release Him, but the Chief Priests cried out, saying, "If you let this man go, you are not Caesar's friend, whoever makes himself a king speaks against Caesar."

When Pilate heard that saying, he brought Yahshua forth, and sat down in judgment seat in a place that is called the "Pavement", but in the Hebrew, "Gabbatha." It was the Preparation Day for the Passover, about the sixth hour, and he said to the Chief Priests, "Behold your King!" But they cried out, "Away with Him. Away with Him, Crucify Him." Pilate said to them, "Shall I crucify your King?" The Chief Priests answered, "We have no king but Caesar."

Then he delivered Him to them to be crucified. They took Yahshua, and removed the purple robe and put His own raiment on Him and led Him away to crucify Him. As they led Him away, they laid hold upon one Simon, a Cyrenian, coming out of the country, the father of Alexander and Rufus, and on him they laid the wooden stake, that he might bear after Yahshua.

There followed Him a great company of people, and of women, who bewailed and lamented Him. Yahshua turning to them said, "Daughters of Jerusalem, weep not for me, but weep for yourselves, and for your children."

"Behold, the days are coming, in which they shall say, 'Blessed are the barren, and the wombs that never bear, and the breasts which never gave suck.' Then shall they begin to say to the mountains, 'Fall on us.' And to the hills, 'Cover us.' For if they do these things in a green tree, what shall be done in the dry?"

When they were come to the place which is called in the Hebrew Golgotha, which is being interpreted as the "Place of the Skull", they crucified Him with two others on either side of Him and with Yahshua in the midst. Pilate wrote a title, and put it on the wooden stake. The writing was, "Yahshua of Nazareth, the King of the Jews."

Many people then read this title for the place where Yahshua was crucified was close to the city. It was written in Hebrew, Greek and Latin. The Chief Priests said to Pilate, "Write not, the King of the Jews. But that He said, 'I am the King of the Jews.'" Pilate answered, "What I have written, I have written."

The soldiers gave Him vinegar to drink mingled with gall. When He had tasted, He would not drink of it, and the Scripture was fulfilled which said, "He was numbered with the transgressors."

And they that passed by railed on Him, wagging their heads, and saying, "Ah, You that would destroy the Temple, and build it in three days, save yourself, and come down from the tree."

Likewise the Chief Priests and the Scribes were also mocking Him and said amongst themselves, "He saved others, Himself He cannot save. Let the Messiah, the King of Israel now descend from the tree that we may see and believe." They that were crucified with Him reviled Him. Then Yahshua said, "Father, forgive them, for they do not know what they do."

The people stood beholding, and the Rulers also with them derided Him saying, "He saved others, let Him save Himself, if He is the Messiah the Chosen One of God."

The soldiers also mocked Him, coming to Him, and offering Him vinegar, and saying, "If you are the King of the Jews, save yourself." One of the malefactors who were hanged railed on Him saying, "If you are the Messiah, save yourself and us."

But the other answering rebuked him saying, "Do you not fear God, seeing you are in the same condemnation? And we indeed justly, for we receive the due reward of our deeds, but this man has done nothing wrong." Then he said to Yahshua." Lord, remember me when you come into your Kingdom."

Yahshua said to him, "Verily, I say to you, today you will be with me in Paradise" Then the soldiers, when they had crucified Yahshua, took His garments, and made four parts, to every soldier a part and also His coat, now the coat was without seam, woven from the top throughout. They said, "Let us not rend it, but cast lots for it, whose it shall be." That the Scriptures might be fulfilled, "They parted my raiment among them and for my vesture they cast lots." These things the soldiers did.

Now there stood by the stake of Yahshua His mother, and His mother's sister, Mary the wife of Cleophas, and Mary Magdalene. When Yahshua saw His mother, and the disciple standing by, whom He loved, He said to His mother, Woman, behold your son! Then He said to the disciple, "Behold your mother!" From that hour that disciple took her to be his own.

Now from the sixth hour there was darkness over all the land to the ninth hour. About the ninth hour Yahshua cried with a loud voice, saying, "Eli, Eli, Lama Sabachthani." That is to say, "My God, My God, Why have You forsaken me?" Some of them that stood there, when they heard said, "This man calls for Elijah."

One man filled a sponge full of vinegar, and put on a reed, and gave Him to drink, others saying, "Let Him alone, let us see whether Elijah will come to take Him down." After this Yahshua knowing that all things were now accomplished, that the Scripture might be fulfilled, said, "I thirst." Yahshua cried again with a loud voice, "It is finished." And He bowed His head and gave up the ghost.

The veil of the Temple was rent in twain from the top to the bottom, and the earth did quake, and the rocks rent, and the graves were opened, and many bodies of the saints who slept arose, and came out of the graves after resurrection, and went into the holy city, and appeared to many.

When the Centurion saw what was done, he glorified God, saying, "Certainly this was a righteous man." All the people that came together to that sight, beholding the things which were done, smote their breasts, and returned.

All His acquaintances, and the women that followed Him from Galilee, among whom was Mary Magdalene, and Mary the mother of James the less and of Joses, and Salome, and the mother of Zebedee's children stood afar off beholding these things.

The Chief Priests, because it was the Preparation Day, that the bodies should not remain upon the tree on the Sabbath, (For that Sabbath was a High Day, the first day of the Feast of Unleavened

Bread), besought Pilate that their legs might be broken, and they might be taken away.

The soldiers came to break the legs of the first, and of the other which was crucified with Him. But when they came to Yahshua and saw that He was already dead did not break His legs, but one of the soldiers pierced His side with a spear, and forthwith came out blood and water.

He that saw bear record and his record is true and he knows that what he says is true, so that you might believe. For these things were done, that the Scripture would be fulfilled, "A bone of Him shall not be broken." And again another Scripture which says, "They shall look on Him whom they have pierced."

When the evening had come, because it was the Preparation Day for the Passover, that is, the day before the Sabbath, the first day of the Feast of Unleavened Bread, Joseph of Arimathea, an honorable counselor, who also waited for the Kingdom of Yahweh, went boldly before Pilate, and craved the body of Yahshua.

Pilate marveled if He was already dead, and calling the Centurion, he asked him whether He had been dead for a while. When he knew of the Centurion that Yahshua was dead, he gave the body to Joseph.

Joseph brought fine linen, and took Him down from the stake. There came also Nicodemus, who at the first came to Yahshua by night, and brought a mixture of myrrh and aloes, about a hundred pounds.

Then they took the body of Yahshua, and wound it in linen clothes with the spices, as the manner of the Jews is to bury their dead. Now in the place where He was crucified was a garden, and in the garden a new sepulcher, wherein was never man yet lay. There they lay Yahshua because of the Day of Preparation for the sepulcher was nigh at hand.

There were women also, which came with Him from Galilee, followed after them, and beheld the sepulcher, and how His body was laid. They returned, and prepared spices and ointments, and rested on the Sabbath according to the commandment concerning the first day of the Feast of Unleavened Bread.

The next day, that followed the Day of Preparation, the Chief Priests and Pharisees came together to Pilate, saying, "Sir, we remember that that deceiver said, while He was yet alive, 'After three days I will rise again.' Command therefore that the sepulcher be made sure until the third day, lest His disciples come by night, and steal Him away, and say to the people, 'He is risen from the dead,' so the last error shall be worse than the first."

Pilate said to them, "You have a watch, go your way and make it as secure as you can." So they went and made the sepulcher sure, sealing the stone and setting a watch.

In the end of the Sabbath, as it began to dawn toward the first of the week there was a great earthquake, for the angel of the Lord descended from heaven, and came and rolled back the stone from the door, and sat upon it. His countenance was like lightning, and his raiment was white as snow, and for fear of him the keepers did shake, and became as dead men.

Some of the watch came into the city, and showed to the Chief Priests all the things that were done. When they were all assembled with the Elders, and had taken counsel, they gave a large sum of money to the soldiers, saying." Say, 'His disciples came by night, and stole Him while we slept.' And if this comes to the governor's ears, we will persuade him, and secure you." So they took the money and did as they were told, and this saying is commonly reported among the Chief Priests and Elders until this day.

CHAPTER XII

As it began to dawn to the first of the week Mary Magdalene came early to the sepulcher, and seeing the stone taken away she ran to Simon Peter, and to the other disciple, whom Yahshua loved, and said to them, "They have taken away the Lord out of the sepulcher, and we don't know where they have laid Him." Peter went forth, and that other disciple, and came to the sepulcher.

Both of them ran together, and the other disciple did outrun Peter, and came first to the sepulcher. And stooping down, saw the linen clothes lying, yet he did not go in. Then Simon Peter, following him went into the sepulcher, and seeing the linen lie, and the napkin, that was about His head, not lying with the linen clothes, but wrapped together in a place by itself.

Then that other disciple, who came first to the sepulcher, went in also and he saw, and believed. For as yet they knew not the Scripture that He must raise again from the dead. The disciples went away again to their own home.

But Mary Magdalene stood without at the sepulcher weeping, and as she wept, she stooped down, and looked into the sepulcher, and seeing two angels in white sitting, and the one at the head, and the other at the feet, where the body of Yahshua had lain.

They said to her, "Woman, why do you weep?" She said to them, "Because they have taken away my Lord, and I know not where they have laid Him." When she had thus said, she turned herself back, and saw Yahshua standing, and knew not that it was Yahshua.

Yahshua said to her, "Woman, why do you weep? Whom do you seek?" She, supposing Him to be the gardener, said to Him, "Sir, if you have born Him away tell me where you have laid Him, and I will take Him away."

Yahshua said to her, "Mary." She turned herself and said to Him, "Rabboni," which is to say, "Master." Yahshua said to her, "Touch me not, for I have not yet ascended to my Father. But go to my brethren, and say to them, 'I ascend to my Father and your Father, and my God, and your God."

Mary Magdalene came and told the disciples that she had seen the Lord, and He had spoken these things to her. When they had heard that He was alive, and had been seen of her, did not believe her.

Now when Yahshua ascended to His Father having taken upon Himself the sins of the world the angel of Yahweh showed me Yahshua, the High Priest, standing before the angel of the Lord, and Satan standing at His right hand to resist Him.

The angel of Yahweh said to Satan, "The Lord rebukes you Satan, even the Lord that has chosen Jerusalem rebukes you. Is not this a brand plucked out of the fire?" Now Yahshua was clothed with filthy garments, and stood before the Lord.

The angel of the Lord spoke to those that stood before Him, saying, "Take away the filthy garments from Him." To Yahshua He said, "Behold, I have caused your iniquity to pass from you and I will clothe you with a change of raiment. So they set a mitre upon His head and clothed Him with garments.

Now upon the first of the week, very early in the morning, at the rising of the sun, Joanna and the mother of James and Salome came to the sepulcher, bringing spices which they had prepared, and certain others came with them. They said among themselves, "Who will roll away the stone from the door of the sepulcher?" When they looked, they saw that the stone was rolled away, for it was very great.

Entering into the sepulcher, they saw a young man sitting on the right side, clothed in a long white garment, and they were afraid. He said to them, "Fear not, for I know you seek Yahshua of Nazareth, who was crucified. Why do you seek the living among the dead? He is not here, but has risen."

"Remember how He spoke to you when He was yet in Galilee, saying, 'The Son of Man must be delivered into the hands of sinful men to be crucified, and the third day rise again?' Come see the place where the Lord lay, and go quickly, and tell His disciples and Peter that He has been raised from the dead. He goes before you into Galilee. There you shall see Him, lo, I have told you."

And they went out quickly, and fled from the sepulcher, for they trembled with fear and great joy and ran quickly to bring His disciples word. As they went, Yahshua met them, saying, "All hail." They came and held Him by the feet, and worshipped Him. Yahshua said to them, "Do not be afraid, go tell my brethren that they go into Galilee, and there shall they see me."

It was Mary Magdalene, and Joanna, and Mary the mother of James, and other women that were with them, who told these things to the apostles. Their words seemed to them as idle tales, and they did not believe them.

Two of them went that same day to a village called Emmaus, which was from Jerusalem threescore furlongs. They talked together of all these things which had happened. It came to pass, that, while they communed and reasoned, Yahshua drew near, and went with them. But their eyes were holden that they should not know Him. He said to them, "What manner of communications are these that you are having with one another, as you walk, and are sad?"

One of them, whose name was Cleopas, answering said to Him, "Are you only a stranger in Jerusalem, and have not known the things which have come to pass there in these days?" He said to them, "What things?" And they said to Him, "Concerning Yahshua of Nazareth, who was a prophet mighty in deed and word before Yahweh and all the people, and how the Chief Priests and our rulers delivered Him to be condemned to death, and have crucified Him."

"But we trusted that it had been He who should have redeemed Israel. And beside all this, today is the third day since these things were done. Yea and certain women also of our company made us astonished, who went early to the sepulcher, and when they did not find His body, they came, saying, that they had also seen a vision of angels, who said that He is alive." Certain of them who were with us went to the sepulcher, and found it even as the women had said, but Him they did not see."

Then He said to them, "O fools, and slow of heart to believe all that the prophets have spoken. Ought not the Messiah to have suffered these things, and to enter into His glory?"

Beginning at Moses and all the prophets, He expounded to them in all the Scriptures the things concerning Him. They drew close to the village where they went, and He made as though He would have gone further, but they constrained Him, saying, "Abide with us, for it is toward evening, and the day is far spent."

He went in to tarry with them. It came to pass, as He sat at meat with them, He took bread, blessed it, and broke it, and gave it to them. Their eyes were opened, and they knew Him, and He vanished out of their sight. They said one to another, "Did not our hearts burn within us while He talked with us by the way, and while He opened to us the Scriptures?"

They rose up the same hour, and returned to Jerusalem, and found the eleven gathered together, and them that were with them, saying, "The Lord is risen indeed, and has appeared to Simon."

They told what things were spoken in the way, and how He was known of them in the breaking of bread. As they spoke, Yahshua stood in the midst of them, and said to them, "Peace to you." But they were terrified and afraid and supposed that they had seen a spirit.

He said to them, "Why are you troubled and why do thoughts arise in your hearts? Behold my hands and my feet that it is I. Handle me, and see, for a spirit does not have flesh and bones, as you can see that I have."

And He upbraided them for their unbelief and hardness of heart, because they did not believe them who had seen Him after He had risen. When He had spoken, He showed them His hands and His feet. While they yet believed not for joy, and wondered, He said to them, "Have you here any meat?" And they gave Him a piece of broiled fish, and of a honey comb. He took and ate before them.

He said to them, "These are the words which I spoke to you, while I was yet with you, that all things must be fulfilled, which were written in the Law of Moses, and the prophets and the Psalms concerning me."

Then He opened their understanding, that they might understand the Scriptures, and said to them, "Thus it is written, and thus it behooved the

Messiah to suffer, and to raise from the dead the third day, and that repentance and remission of sins should be preached in His Name among all nations, beginning at Jerusalem. You are witnesses of these things."

"Behold, I send the promise of my Father upon you, but tarry in the city of Jerusalem until you are endued with power from on high. Then Yahshua said to them once again, "Peace to you, as the Father has sent me, even so send I you." When He had said this, He breathed on them and said to them, "Receive the Holy Spirit."

But Thomas, one of the twelve, called Didymus, was not with them when Yahshua came. The other disciples said to him, "We have seen the Lord." But he said to them, "Except I see in His hands the print of the nails, and put my finger into the print of the nails, and thrust my hand into His side, I will not believe."

After eight days His disciples were again within, and Thomas was with them, came Yahshua, the doors being shut, and stood in the midst and said, "Peace to you." Then He said to Thomas, "Reach hither your finger, and behold my hands, and reach hither your hand, and thrust it into my side, and be not faithless, but believing." Thomas answering said to Him, "My Lord and my God." Yahshua said to him, "Thomas, because you have seen me, you have believed, blessed are they that have not seen, and have believed."

After these things Yahshua showed Himself again to the disciples at the Sea of Tiberias, and on this wise showed Himself. They were together Simon Peter, Thomas called Didymus, Nathanael of Cana in Galilee, the sons of Zebedee, and two other disciples. Simon Peter said to them, "I am going fishing." They said to him, "We will also go with you."

They went forth, and immediately entered into a ship, and that night they caught nothing. When it was morning, Yahshua stood on the shore, but the disciples did not know that it was Yahshua. Yahshua said to them, "Children, Do you have any meat?" They answered Him, "No." He said to them, "Cast your net on the right side of the ship, and you will find."

They cast their nets as He commanded them and now they were not able to draw it in for the multitude of fishes caught in the net. That disciple whom Yahshua loved said to Peter, "It is the Lord." Now when Simon Peter heard that it was the Lord, he put on his fishers coat (for he was naked), and cast himself into the sea.

The other disciples came in a little ship, (For they were not far from land, as it were, two hundred cubits), dragging the net with fishes. As soon then as they came to land, they saw a fire of coals there, fish laid thereon, and some bread.

Yahshua said to them, "Bring of the fish which you have caught." Simon Peter went up, and drew the net to land full of great fishes, a hundred fifty three, and for all there were so many, yet the net did not break. Yahshua said to them, "Come and dine." None of the disciples dared to ask Him, "Who are you?" They already knew that it was the Lord.

Yahshua came and took bread, and gave them, and fish likewise. This is now the third time that Yahshua showed Himself to His disciples after He had risen from the dead. After they had dined, Yahshua said to Simon Peter, "Simon, son of Jonas, Do you love me more than these?" He said to Him, "Yea, Lord, you know that I love you." He said to him, "Feed my lambs."

He said to him again the second time, "Simon, son of Jonas, Do you love me?" He said to Him, "Lord, you know that I love you." He said to him, "Feed my sheep." He said to him the third time, "Do you love me?" He said to Him, "Lord, you know all things. You know that I love you." Yahshua said to him "Feed my sheep."

"Verily, verily, I say to you, 'When you were young, you clothed yourself, and walked where you would, but when you are old, you will stretch forth your hands, and another shall clothe you, and carry where you would not go." This He spoke, signifying by what death he should glorify Yahweh.

And when He had spoken this, He said to him, "Follow me." Peter, turning about, seeing the disciple whom Yahshua loved following, who also leaned on His breast at supper, and said, "Lord, which is he that will betray you?" Peter seeing him said to Yahshua, "Lord, what about this man?" Yahshua said to him, "If I will that he tarry till I come, what is that to you. Follow me." Then went this saying abroad among the brethren, that this disciple would not die, yet Yahshua did not say to him that He shall not die, but, "If I will that he tarry till I come, what is that to you?"

They asked of Him, saying, "Lord, will you at this time restore again the Kingdom of Israel?" He said to them, "It is not for you to know the things or the seasons, which the Father has put in His own power. But you shall receive power, after that the Holy Spirit has come upon you, and you shall be witnesses to me in Jerusalem, in all of Judea, in Samaria, and into the uttermost parts of the earth."

The eleven disciples went away into Galilee, into a mountain where Yahshua had appointed them to go. And when they saw Him, they worshipped Him. Yahshua came and spoke to them, saying, "All power is given to me in heaven and in earth. Go into the entire world, and preach the gospel to every creature. He that believes and is baptized will be saved, but he that does not believe will be damned."

"And these signs will follow them that believe. In my Name they will cast out devils, they shall speak with new tongues, they shall take up serpents, and if they drink any deadly thing, it will not hurt them. They will lay hands on the sick and they shall recover. Go therefore, and teach all nations, baptizing them in my Name for the remission of sin, teaching them to observe all things whatsoever I have commanded you and, lo, I am with you always to the end of the world."

So then, after Yahshua had spoken to them, it came to pass, while He blessed them He was parted from them, and received up into Heaven, and sat on the right hand of Yahweh.

While His disciples looked steadfastly toward Heaven, as He went up, behold, two men stood by them in white apparel, who also said, "You men of Galilee, why do you stand gazing up into Heaven? This same Yahshua who is taken up from you into heaven, shall so come in like manner as you have seen Him go into Heaven."

And there are also many other things which Yahshua did in the presence of His disciples, which are not written in this book, which, if they should be written every one, I suppose that even the world itself could not contain the books that should be written. But these are written that you might believe that Yahshua is the Messiah, the Son of Yahweh, and that believing you might have eternal life through His Name.

The Revelation of Yahshua the Messiah: "Behold, He comes with clouds, and every eye shall see Him, and they which pierced Him, and all kindreds of the earth will wail because of Him.

The Lord says, "I am Alpha and Omega, the beginning and the ending, which is, and which was, and which is to come, the Almighty." I saw heaven opened, and behold a white horse, and He that sits upon him is called, "Faithful and True" and in righteousness He judges and makes war.

His eyes are as a flame of fire, and on His head He has many crowns, and He has a Name written, that no man knows, but He Himself. He is clothed with a vesture dipped in blood, and His Name is called "The Word of Yahweh." The armies of Heaven follow Him upon white horses, clothed with fine linen, white and clean.

And out of His mouth goes a sharp sword, that with it He will smite the nations, and He will rule them with a rod of iron. He treads the winepress of the fierceness and wrath of Almighty God. On His vesture and on His thigh He has a Name written, "King of kings, and Lord of lords." And the Lord will be King over all the earth. In that day there will be one Lord and His Name one.

This shall be the plague whereby Yahweh will smite all the people that have fought against Jerusalem. Their flesh will consume away while they stand upon their fee, and their eyes shall consume away in their holes, and their tongues will consume away in their mouths.

So shall it be that every one that is left of all the nations which come against Jerusalem shall even go up from year to year to worship the King, the Lord of hosts and to keep the Feast of Tabernacles.

It shall come to pass that whoever will not come up of all the families of the earth to Jerusalem to worship the King, the Lord of hosts, even upon them shall be no rain, there shall be the plague of Egypt, wherewith the Lord will smite the heathen that do not come up to keep the Feast of Tabernacles.

I saw a New Jerusalem and a New Earth, for the first heaven and the first earth had passed away, and there was no more sea. I saw the New Jerusalem, coming down from Yahweh out of Heaven, prepared as a bride adorned for her husband.

And I heard a great voice out of Heaven saying, "Behold, the Tabernacle of Yahweh is with men, and He will dwell with them, and they shall be His people, and Yahweh Himself will be with them, and will be their God."

"And Yahweh shall wipe away all the tears from their eyes, and there shall be no more death, neither sorrow, nor crying, neither shall there be any more pain. For the former things will be passed away."

And the Spirit and the Bride say "Come", and let him that hears say, "Come." Let him that is athirst come. And whosoever will, let him take of the water of life freely. And the Bride prepared herself for the coming of the Lord.

I, Yahshua have sent mine angel to testify to you these things. I am the root and offspring of David, the Bright and Morning Star. He who testifies these things says, "Surely I come quickly." Even so my Lord Yahshua, come quickly. Amen.

Ray Looker
(1940 -   )

Biography

Ray Looker is a Disciple of Yahshua the Messiah, an Apostle of the Messianic Jewish faith and has been a Professor of Theology. Ray is committed to preparing the Church for the coming of the Messiah.

Ray spent 14 years in the U.S. Army as a Senior-Ranking Non-Commissioned Officer. His military assignments took him to Greenland, Germany, Norway and Vietnam. He served in seven major campaigns in Vietnam, and has spent over 30 years as a Missionary and Professor in Europe, China and the inner-cities of America. With graduate degrees in Law Ray worked as a Law Clerk in a Public Defender's Office and with a District Court Judge while doing post-graduate work for a Doctor of Theology Degree.

His post-Doctorate research in Educational and Motivational Psychology allowed him to be a Program Manager in an epidemiological study of mental illness for the Department of Health and Mental Retardation for the State. He later served as a Director of Compliance enforcing a Federal Court

Order on a maximum security prison for the criminally insane, a Justice of the Peace, a Notary Public and as an Auxiliary Police Officer in the State of New York.

Ray ran for the House of Delegates and as a Magistrate with the idea that government 'servants' were to be held accountable to the people for their actions. Ray has also served as Pastor in a Christian Church, and as Messianic Rabbi in a Messianic Jewish Congregation. He has also ministered on both radio and television and has been a Baritone Soloist in various churches when asked to do so.

When the Messiah comes, all men will be required to observe the Commandments of Yahweh, and to keep His Sabbaths, the New Moons, and the Dietary Laws of the written TORAH. Ray's work and ministry is to prepare and to teach Believers the importance of keeping Yahweh's laws and commandments in accordance with His wishes and desires for us.

To raise up the 'Tabernacle of David' in preparation for the coming of the Lord, the Church must rebuild and restore Christianity upon the bedrock foundation of the Apostles and Prophets, which is the written Torah.

Ray's first book on "Judeo-Christianity" began his journey into the Messianic Jewish faith.

His many books on the Messianic Movement of the Holy Spirit are a testimony of the dedication of his life to preparing the way for the coming of the Messiah. As he is able, he intends to make these books available on the internet for worldwide access to everyone everywhere.

Made in the USA
Las Vegas, NV
08 December 2023

82386493R00142